The Secret

René Fumoleau

The Secret

The best stories
are yet
to be lived.

R. Fumoleau

NOVALIS

Cover and interior design: Christiane Lemire

Cover design based on photos by Erica Humbert-Droz and Claude Gravel

Author's photo: Alex Czarnecki, Yellowknife, North West Territories

Layout: Christiane Lemire

Editors: Fred Miller and Bernadette Gasslein

Business Office: Novalis, 49 Front Street East, 2nd floor, Toronto, Ontario M5E 1B3; 1-800-387-7164; Toronto and outside Canada (416) 363-3303

ISBN: 2-890889-19-X

Printed in Canada

Canadian Cataloguing in Publication

Fumoleau, René

The secret

Poems.

ISBN 2-890889-19-X

1. Title

PS8561.U8875S43 1997 C811'.54 C97-901192-2

PR9199.3.F85S43 1997

Table of Contents

Editor's Foreword

by
Bernadette Gasslein

Like a parable, René Fumoleau stalks our imagination: A story here, a poem there, innocent at first. Then, with a sleight of word that boggles the imagination, he upends our world. The North, that distant fringe of Canadian society, becomes the central prism through which reality is probed. Folks who normally inhabit the edge occupy centre stage. The same oral quality that marks the gospel parables marks Fumoleau's work. Don't just read it. Listen to it; read it aloud with a friend, a lover—and enjoy the effects.

Take, for example, "Too Independent." Fred and Cathy become "a problem" to a system unable to see its own stupidity and limitation and, after a deadpan exchange with the official sent to deal with the "problem," we hear the official grudgingly admit that he wants to be "free like them."

One of the most striking examples of the world turned upside down is presented in "Pagan Woman." As elsewhere in Fumoleau's work, a woman is the bearer of insight. In a radical turning of the tables, Christ himself is healed by the love that flows between him and the Syro-Phonenician woman: "She delivered me from the demon of simply repeating the past ... she gave me the whole world." Love is at the heart of this transformation, as elsewhere, for "doctrines, miracles, feelings and discussions cannot spark faith."

Over and over again, as the friends who have known this Oblate priest, missionary, author and photographer over the forty-odd years he has spent in the North have come to expect, Fumoleau colours outside the lines. In "Sins" he makes us grapple with a different angle on tradition and locked doors. Lock doors if you will, but look out: you can hear "the Other Intelligence trying the doorknob" (Thomas Johnson). The absurdity of southern, bureaucratic approaches, one of Fumoleau's dominant themes, emerges in sharp contrast to the wisdom of a Dene elder: "Have you ever heard of anybody building a bridge by starting at the centre?"

And, for Fumoleau, "Nice" is the ultimate four-letter word. In this poem, the good and pious will scramble for cover as Fumoleau hits straight to the heart of religion—or any other way of being—that has no teeth.

"The Secret" typifies the Fumoleau approach. Here the world of René Fumoleau draws us into its embrace: graceful, deeply felt, distinctive, different thought. Fumoleau's insights, like the women of whom he writes here and elsewhere, disturb our peace of mind and arouse familiar—or unfamiliar—longings. We might want to get rid of those feelings, but he never lets us escape into the world of the lifeless, the robotic, the shallow or the senseless. Paradoxically, he rejects one secret, and instead gives us another. But, of course, to discover the secret, we must do with his poems as we would with the parables: read another and another and another …

Preface

Do you believe in New Year's resolutions? Usually I don't, but in early January, 1997, I looked ahead: "I have already drafted or written many short stories. February will be very cold but sunny, the perfect weather for writing. I will dedicate the month to story writing. In the following months I can write in a more leisurely way. Then, in fall, I can publish a sequel to *Here I Sit*."

In the last week in January, I cleaned my desk and office, my mind all geared up to February 1. And guess what? On the morning of January 31, my old laptop computer started to whine. By evening it had succumbed to a terminal illness.

A wise person stays cool in every situation. I realized I was not yet a wise person: "If the Evil Spirit plays that trick on me, I can manage. But if it is a call from my Good Spirit, to what is he calling me?"

That January 31 evening was the calmest ever. The stunted spruce trees and the lonely birch tree behind my house whispered to me: "Everything is O.K." At midnight, a fierce gale blew in from the Barren Lands. The trees bent and swayed in every direction, but they still smiled: "Everything is O.K." As for me, I was still panicky.

Three months previously, a friend had offered me his old computer, similar to mine, which he wanted to retire. I had replied. "Thank you, but mine is still working well." Regret surfaced: "If only I had ..." "When Antonio was in Yellowknife ..." "Last time I was in Edmonton I could have ..."

A friend offered to find me the newest computer with pleiades of programs and a galaxy of options. Really, I didn't need a Cadillac of a computer or even a Harley Davidson. I only wanted a plain, old pushbike. But how to find the most simple in a world where anything three months old is obsolete? So, after one or two wrong decisions, I gave up my fall publishing dream and I fell into a literary sleep.

Five weeks later, I happened to open a file of sixty-some letters my friends had written after the release of *Here I Sit.*

I reread a letter from Saskatchewan: "Considering the mystery of the human mind and the infinite variety of available choices, the ending of your 'Photograph' story is plausible." A week later another Saskatchewan resident had written: "Sometimes I am one of the persons in your 'Photograph' story; sometimes I am the other one."

All letters had delighted me, especially when readers had discovered much more in a story than I had put into it myself. Half of what I learned from *Here I Sit* I learned from readers' comments.

I kept reading:

"You sure know how to excite a young family ..."
"Great realist and humourist of life in the North ..."
"Livre aussi pertinent qu'impertinent ..."
"The wisdom of people close to the earth ..."
"Continuez à nous secouer en nous berçant tendrement ..."
"Your words help me see a span of my life in a new light ..."
"Sharp-edged, wry, deep, funny, light and serious ..."
"Your viewpoint is unique, unsentimental, non-judging ..."
"Textes doux et puissants, genre tigre en sieste ..."
"An excellent springboard for meditation ..."
"Emerveillé de l'humour, de la simplicité, et de la sagesse ..."
"Your book is 'some good' as us Newfoundlanders say ..."
"Quelle merveilleuse présentation artistique, très Zen ..."

I had started to read your comments for distraction and, suddenly, you were again sending me on a voyage of self-discovery, revealing to me my fears and my hopes, my dislikes and my loves, those yet unknown and those already forgotten.

Well, my friends, I simply gulped down your bait, all the way to my heart. I retrieved my old files, drafts, notes, clippings and references. By then an Edmonton friend had sent me his old laptop and I started to write again. Thank you all for your wake-up call.

René Fumoleau

Sins

After living for a few months of 1953
  with the K'ashot'ine of Rádęlı̨ Kǫ́ (Fort Good Hope),
  I was teaching the Ten Commandments.
You know them: love God, honour your parents,
  don't kill, don't steal, don't lie,
  and don't commit adultery.

I explained:

"It is a sin
  to do what we shouldn't do,
  or not to do what we should do.
Sins are rated as big or small.
What do you think is the worst sin of all?"

The ten Dene discussed together,
  and after a while Radisca explained to me:

"We talked it over, and we all agree:
The worst sin people can make
  is to lock their door."

Useless

Bill and Gail and their three children live in Edmonton.

Bill is a maintenance man
who doesn't make much money,
but enough for the family.
Twice he refused a better paying job
which would have meant less time at home.

Gail sews some of the family's clothes.
—But she prevents the garment industry
from reaping huge profits from cheap Asian labour.

They grow vegetables in their backyard
and produce about two-thirds of their needs.
They say a garden is more fun than a lawn.
—But how will Safeway and Supersave prosper
if more families become self-sufficient?

Gail prepares nutritious meals herself.
—But, with more people like her,
the packaging industry
(which makes more profit than the farmers)
would have to pack up.

My friends don't speculate on the land and the housing market.
With the help of a few friends,
they renovated an old house.
—But, by not hiring architects and tradespeople,
they slowed down the city's economy.

They bought second-hand furniture
which turned out to be functional and beautiful.
—With more Gails and Bills,
what would happen to IKEA and The Brick Warehouse?

Their car takes them wherever they want to go,
even if it's the oldest one on the block.
—These people really don't care
about the welfare of Ford, G.M., or Toyota.

The children don't waste money on candies or junk food.
—If all children were like them,
how could dentists afford new yachts?
Too bad for the yacht builders, too.

The family has a canoe, and for their holidays,
they drive to a lake, or to the mountains,
and camp by themselves or with a few friends.
—They don't even worry about not supporting
fancy hotels and foreign airlines.

Gail and Bill volunteer some of their time
with a few neighbourhood organizations.
They manage to save and to send money
to Oxfam and Development and Peace
to promote the self-reliance of people
in what we call the Third world, the oppressed one.

They certainly have their ups and downs,
but parents and children trust each other,
communicate with great openness,
give freedom to each other,
and enjoy each other's company.
—Really too bad for psychologists, counsellors,
psychiatrists and welfare officers,
whose services they have never required.

Betty, the seventeen-year-old,
has never been arrested for drunkenness
or for possession of drugs or stolen goods,
and she hasn't smashed up a car yet.
She doesn't bring prosperity to
lawyers, prosecutors, police officers,
and to builders of beautiful jails,
court houses and police headquarters.

They are allergic to greed,
They don't lust mindlessly for money,
and they don't worship the Gross National Product.
They believe that markets exist to serve people,
not the other way around.
—But how could banks build magnificent offices
if people didn't need loans and mortgages,
and didn't pay high interest on credit cards?

I'm telling you,
in our society of consumerism and commercialism,
my friends are so useless!

Two Worlds

When Albert set a fishnet in winter,
his ice chisel danced as in a ballet.
Saw, axe, pliers, hammer, screwdriver
worked as if parts of his hands.
He had built two log cabins in the bush,
and a modern house in T'èʔehda (Dettah).
He prepared nutritious meals
on an electric range or on the crudest campfire.
When his wife lay sick in hospital for three months,
Albert sat at the old sewing machine
and sewed clothes for their children.
He could drive his canoe through ten kilometres of fog,
and land three hundreds metres from his aim.
Prospecting and mining companies hired him to stake claims
or to operate any kind of heavy equipment.
His forecasts were as accurate as any weather office's
and he had a direct line to all animals:

"I'm going moose hunting.
There was quite a storm four days ago,
then hot for two days,
and it rained yesterday.
The bull moose which was near Neyah Lake
must have gone North,
and moved to that open pasture
near the Black River's second bend.
I'll go and get it."

But Albert couldn't read or write:

"René, I've got those papers in the mail;
must be from the government.
What do they want?"

"Not much to worry about.
Some information about your youngest child."

"Can we go tomorrow to the Laing building,
    and fix it?"

The five-storey Laing building had been erected
    when the N.W.T. government and administration
    moved from Ottawa to Yellowknife in 1967.
We rode the elevator to the third floor
    and to the office concerned with the child.
Albert easily answered the clerk's inquiry.

Obviously, Albert had never been there.
He walked cautiously, as on a bush trail,
    watching calmly to the left and to the right,
    used to paying attention to every sign in nature.

"Albert, do you feel like visiting the other floors?"

In those days, computers had not yet reached Denendeh.
Officers and clerks were writing or typewriting memos,
    surveys' conclusions, or government's secrets.
Others deeply pondered new policies
    or read books or sheaves of documents.
Albert's mind, no doubt, recorded every detail.

We climbed to the fifth floor, the executive domain,
    more awesome with its thick carpets,
    Eskimo carvings, original paintings,
    fancier furniture and more elegant clothing.

We toured every floor, and stood in the lobby.
Albert seemed to be as happy
    as any explorer discovering a new land, but:

"René, they told me
    that there are people working in that building.
Where are they?"

Shanghai

We were seven friends on a trip through the Far East.
We landed in Shanghai early one morning,
    and we had to wait for another plane in the afternoon.
We had been travelling for a few days already,
    and my friends decided to rest in a hotel.

I took off by myself to visit the city,
    a whole new world to see, to hear, to smell:
    people, clothes, streets, bicycles,
    odours, colours, and melodic languages.
Fascinated and dizzy with excitement,
    I wandered, looked, listened, marvelled,
    and tasted fruits with unknown names.

I reached an open market in an enormous square.
Exotic merchandise and mysterious goods were displayed
    in bags and baskets, on tables and on the ground.
A gate, decorated with rich colours and signs,
    led me through a wall to a larger market place
    still more attractive and alluring.

I looked at my watch. Is it really so late?
I must go back to the hotel right away!
Then, I started to panic when I realized
    I didn't even know the name of the hotel,
    or what street it was on.

I flagged a cabdriver who, luckily, spoke some English:

> "I know what my hotel looks like, but not the address.
> You know the hotels where most of the foreigners stay?
> If you drive me around I will recognize it."

Off we went, through many streets and more avenues.

"No, it's not here ... it's not this one either."

After many turns south, north and all around:

"That's the one!"

I gave the driver what I thought was a good tip.
My six friends were in the lobby, with our luggage:

"You're just in time, we're leaving for the airport."

Did we catch our flight? I do not know
because I woke up from my dream
before we reached the airport.

But ... I truly lived that dream many times in my life.

Parish Life

"My dear brothers and sisters,

I am new in your parish, but I've learned already
    that long and exacting working hours
    strain numerous family relationships.
Many husbands, wives, parents and children suffer
    because they have little time
    to talk, to laugh and to play together.
Yes, my friends,
    you need time to relax, time to smell the flowers,
    time to rejoice with the Creator in creation,
    time to build up happy family relationships.

As your parish priest, I want to teach you
    that work is less important
    than relationships and celebrations.

To channel all my energy towards such a goal
    I gave up my parents, my brothers and my sisters,
    and I renounced marriage and children.
Now, I will also forgo rest and vacations
    so that I can work for you twenty-four hours a day,
    weekdays, Sundays and holidays."

Pagan Woman

Mark 7: 24-30
Matthew 15: 21-28

My apostles are probably asleep,
and, this evening, I am happy to be by myself.
The day was not too hard,
but I need to sort out my thoughts and my feelings.

At noon, the Canaanite woman stood in front of me,
her eyes both soft and fiery,
without arrogance, but confident in herself:

"Have mercy on me!
My daughter has a demon
and she is in terrible condition."

"I am sorry,
but I have been sent only to the people of Israel.
It is not right to take the children's bread
and to throw it to the dogs."

"Yes, but the dogs under the table
eat the crumbs that fall down."

That was more than confidence;
she vibrated with pure faith.
She doesn't know anything about our beliefs,
but she forced me to have faith in her.
I discovered her own worth and the greatness of her life,
and I said "Yes."

She thanked me sincerely, without platitude,
and she returned to her daughter.
Then, Peter, always full of common sense:

"Jesus, what's happening to you?
This pagan, a Syro-Phoenician,
she belongs to the people
whom the LORD ordered us to destroy.
There she was, demanding favours
which are reserved for the LORD's chosen ones.
What pretention, trying to explain to you
what you should do or should not do!"

Peter, he can see through everything!

I, too, I was shocked.
I thought I knew everything about the LORD,
who He is and what He wants.
Then, this woman ventured to tell me
that the LORD loves pagans as much as Jews,
and that they also have some right to his blessings.

Manahat, the scholar, turned inquisitor:

"Jesus, will you question everything,
even the LORD's predilection for us?
Are you going to preach that the LORD
wants to make a covenant with all nations?
If the pagans also are the LORD's children,
if it is enough to adore Him in spirit and in truth,
then, who will need us, Scribes,
Pharisees, and Doctors of the Law?"

Yes, I know.
All the laws and ordinances
which they have fabricated and compiled
are quite useful, aren't they?
At least, they help control the ordinary people.

Eleazar, the levite, was inflamed:

"Jesus, do you pretend that pagans
don't need to read the Torah,
or to sacrifice goats and bullocks?
Then, why is it necessary for us?
Jesus, if you break only one link of the chain,
there will be chaos, despair, anarchy.
Everything will crumble, even the Temple."

Once minds had cooled off a bit,
John looked me in the eyes:

"Jesus, there must have been a lot of love
flowing between you and her.
Otherwise, she couldn't have found the right words,
and you, you would never have understood her."

He was right, John.
Doctrines, miracles, feelings and discussions
cannot spark faith.

And I, without that woman,
I would probably have remained
only a good disciple of the Baptist,
or a professor with a mummified message.
I would have sidestepped my mission.
I would not have discovered who I must be.

Life cannot be taught,
but events guide me on my way to becoming Jesus:
John's baptism, lake storms, wheat sowing,
Cana, Capernaum, Bethsaida,
Jairus, lepers, tax collectors,
And today, that pagan woman and her invitation:

Live a new creation every day,
become conscious of who you are,
move ahead of your vision to accomplish it,
... even if fidelity requires rupture.

Yes, she was right.
Without risk, spiritual life withers and dies.

Tonight, that woman and her daughter must be full of joy,
    as I am full of joy: How much I owe her!
She delivered me
    from the demon of simply repeating the past,
    from an easy satisfaction with only the children of Israel.
I had enough with Palestine,
    she gave me the whole world.

The night is so dark,
    the Light so brilliant.

Thank you, pagan woman!

Nobody

"I was passing by,
    and I wondered about the sign above your door:
        'Working Together.'"

"This is an Employment Centre and I am the Director.
Do you have a job?"

"I listen to people, I give them hope.
I help them to discover their own worth."

"Are you a registered counsellor?
How much do you charge per hour?"

"I charge nothing, I just share of what I am."

"So you don't contribute to the Gross National Product.
Do you receive federal assistance?"

"Me and my friends, we manage.
People help us too."

"What friends are you talking about?"

"Simon, Andrew, James, John,
    Martha, Mary Magdalene."

"What kind of family is that!
Have you ever had a real job?"

"I was a carpenter, a good one too."

"Why did you quit?"

"I have other things to do with my life."

"Like what?"

"Trying to empower the people I meet,
    helping the sick to strengthen their faith
    so that they can heal."

"Are you trying
    to put doctors out of business?
If everybody worked for nothing
    money would never go around and around
    and create more wealth.
Do you have a car?"

"People can be fully alive when walking
    as well as when driving."

"Do you and your friends belong to a union?"

"Yes, the People of Good Will."

"Is your union registered?
O.K., I'll make it clear to you:
The government promised jobs, jobs, jobs,
    and it must deliver jobs before the next election.
My own quota is to create forty jobs in two months,
    and I'm afraid that you won't be on my list.
Are you trying to undermine government policies?"

"I tell people:
    'Give to the government what belongs to the government,
    but don't give up your freedom and your dignity.'"

"Let me check the files of the Security Services.
Your name is not even on our computer!
No university, no bank accounts, no credit cards?
No R.R.S.P., no shares, no saving bonds?
You don't even belong to Diners Club?
Man, you're a nobody, you don't exist."

"Oh yes, I do. I belong to the real world."

"You like word games, don't you?
My assessment? You are truly unemployable
    and you will never be an asset to society.
Fortunately, you're not a dangerous person;
    who will ever listen to your dreams?
Here's the address of a renowned psychiatrist.
If anyone can help you back to reality, he's the one.
Goodbye and good luck ... You need it."

"Do not worry for me, sir, I am the Way."

Mr. Fix-It

Two men struggled with their car engine.
Armed with a wrench and a screwdriver,
they pried here, checked there,
lifted this, and loosened that.

Father Albert, the parish priest, walked by:

"You've got problems?"

"Father, we checked the plugs, the starter,
the battery, the carburetor, the whole thing,
but she won't go."

"Boys, there's an easy way.
Pray to God, and He'll help you."

"You're kidding!
God is not a mechanic."

"No, but He's all powerful.
Let's kneel down on the grass
and say the Our Father together.
And make sure you pray with all your heart."

They did.

"O.K., boys, get into your car,
start the engine, and have a good trip."

They started the car so easily
and they shifted into gears so rapidly
that they hardly had time to shout back:

"Thank you, Father."

Father Albert fell on his knees,
trembling and sobbed:

"Oh, my! Oh, my!
If I ask my God for something,
and my God gives it to me,
I'd better start searching for the true God."

I.O.U.

For thousands of years,
the Denesǫłıné (Chipewyans) controlled the Barren Land
from the Rocky Mountains to Hudson Bay:

"The lakes were full of whitefish and fifty-pound trout.
At times, the land offered very little,
but now and then we were surrounded by caribou.
We bartered among ourselves,
or with the neighbouring tribes.
I guess we were rich but we didn't know it."

In the early 1800s, fur traders brought
tea, flour, sugar, tobacco, copper kettles,
beads, buttons, woven cloth, twine gill nets,
guns, needles, scissors, and steel knives:

"The Hudson's Bay Company didn't use cash.
Southern goods were priced in terms of furs,
and a 'Made Beaver' was the unit of trade.
A kettle was so many 'Made Beavers,'
an axe, so many 'Made Beavers.'
For a gun we piled up furs as high as the gun,
even if some guns exploded after only a few shots."

In fall, every Dene purchased on credit
what his family needed for the trapping season.
The trader knew who was a good reliable trapper.
Months later the trapper spread his furs on the counter:

"The manager said, 'I'll give you so much,'
and we couldn't argue with him.
He cancelled our previous debt and he said:
'Now you have so much on your account.'
If we stayed a bit around the trading post,
it was easy to spend it all,
and the manager said: 'Now you have debts.'"

In 1900, the Dene saw their first dollar bills ever:

"The government Treaty Commissioner
gave five dollars to every Dene,
and a bit more to the chief and councillors.
When we go and visit another village
we always bring some presents,
so we guessed the commissioner did as we do.
Later on, the government told us
that the money was to buy our land,
but no Dene would ever sell their land."

The debt policy invented by the fur traders
and the cash system brought by the government
have grown branches in every Dene community,
and they well match the Western "Buy Now—Pay Later":

"Ernie, I want to fly to Yellowknife today.
Can you lend me fifty dollars?"

"You have no money? How come?"

"Yes, I had money, but I lent fifty dollars to Julia.
She had no money for bingo last night."

"Julia had no money? How come?"

"Yes, she had money, but she lent fifty dollars
to Baptist who needed gas for his truck."

"Baptist had no money? How come?"

"Yes, he had money, but he lent fifty dollars
to Patricia who needed a new dress."

"Patricia had no money? How come?"

"Yes, she had money, but she lent fifty dollars
to Jimmy, her dad, who needed skidoo parts."

"Jimmy had no money? How come?"

"Yes, he had money, but he lent fifty dollars
to his brother Alphonse to pay his phone bill."

"Alphonse had no money? How come?"

"Yes, he had money, but he lent fifty dollars to Gina.
She was a bit short to buy a radio."

"Gina had no money? How come?"

"Yes, she had money, but she lent fifty dollars to Pete,
who was going to Edmonton for a meeting."

"Pete had no money? How come?"

"Yes, he had money, but he lent *you* fifty dollars.
So now, *you* can lend *me* fifty dollars."

Independence

"Our ancestral tribes and our Dene Nation
    have always been independent and self-sufficient."

"I know it, but the Department of Indian Affairs
    wants you to prove it."

"So, what should we do?"

"You need to hire a few white people:
    a fund raiser.
    a finance manager,
    a planning consultant."

"What will they do?"

"They'll prepare a budget and a set of guidelines."

"What is that budget for?"

"So that you can hire a few more white people:
    linguists, lawyers, economists, cartographers,
    office managers, anthropologists, media experts,
    computer analysts, political consultants,
    constitutional advisors ... and a few others."

"Why do we need all those people?
What will they do?"

"They'll do research, organize consultations,
    prepare reports, and summarize conclusions.
In the end, they will prove to the government
    that you have always been
    an autonomous and self-sufficient nation."

"But if we need all those people,
    we won't be self-sufficient any more."

"Yes, my friend,
    and the Department of Indian Affairs knows it well."

Ignacia

Augusto led me up and down narrow mountain paths.
After an hour, we reached the village of Lacmaan
  hanging on the slopes of the Filipino Cordillera
  among pine trees, bamboo trees and banana trees.

The splendour of the large valley enchanted me.
The songs of birds, pigs, dogs and roosters filled my ears.
I was awed by the genius of the Applay tribal people
  who, through dozens of generations,
  have built rice terraces along the mountain slopes,
  and devised a complex irrigation system.

In the first hut we entered,
  Ignacia, with genuine Filipino hospitality,
  served us rice, potatoes, eggs, fruit and coffee.

In the front yard, a dozen small hens
  went about their business of eating and fattening up.
Repeatedly they scratched the dust with their claws,
  picked up tiny seeds, pieces of grass, grains of sand,
  and whatever they knew formed a proper diet.

Ignacia added a treat to the hens' menu.
She brought a glass bowl full of rice,
  and spread handfuls of grain on the ground.
The hens, with astonishing swiftness
  and sharper eyesight than mine,
  picked up one grain after another.
They turned, twisted, shifted right and left,
  side by side, but ignoring each other.

A rooster, twice the size of the hens,
  and adorned with a flaming red comb,
  arrogantly pushed his way among the hens.
He picked up two or three grains,
  but he was more interested in picking on the hens.

With self-proclaimed superiority, and using his beak as a lance,
he threw himself at one hen, at another one,
and even pounced on three or four together.
In the best—or worst—spirit of competition,
he proclaimed that the world belongs to the strong,
that there is no place for the weak
and that the winner should take all.

Ignacia chased the rooster away.
Again and again, he came back.
Again and again, Ignacia chased him away.
Only after the hens had enjoyed a reasonable meal
did she allow the rooster into the feeding area.

Watching the rooster amid such a flurry of animosity
made me feel that animals behave like people.
Or is it people who behave like animals?

Fortunately, there are many Ignacias in the world.

Gate

Manila's Aurora Avenue,
between Katipunan and Cubao,
is mostly a succession of grey walls,
small shops, vacant lots, rundown buildings,
and faded colours mixed with dirt and garbage:
a common situation in countries
whose resources are plundered by foreigners.

Joint national, provincial and municipal elections
were called for May 11, 1992.
Each of the 32 million Filipino voters
was invited to write 35 names
on the 55-centimetre long ballot
to choose the president, the vice-president,
24 senators, 205 members of parliament,
73 provincial governors and vice-governors,
620 provincial board members,
1,602 mayors, and 13,044 municipal councillors.

Suddenly, Aurora Avenue looked like an art gallery
or a maple tree forest in the fall.
Every night, armies of volunteers or paid labourers
glued colourful posters, new slogans,
new promises on the walls,
and often superimposed each other's artwork.

An iron gate on Aurora Avenue
protected the yard and the mansion
of Patrizio and Sabrina Cabreros.
They became angry when their gate
turned blue and red one night,
yellow and green the next,
when photos of Lopez and Sarmiento
regularly replaced those of Tattao and Quebral,
and vice versa.

Patrizio and Sabrina waited silently in their yard.
Near midnight, they quietly opened the side door,
    and directed their flashlight beam
    onto a man, a bundle of posters and a glue pot:

"What the heck are you doing here?"

"Putting up posters."

"But this is our gate."

"I'm not taking it away from you."

"You're damaging our gate."

"They're only posters."

"We don't want those posters."

"I'm paid 20 pesos a night to put up posters,
    and that's the only work I can find."

"Why don't you go somewhere else?"

"I'm paid to work on Aurora Avenue."

"Holy ... Look at our splendid gate!"

"Forgive me, madame, you, too, sir,
    but I am one of the nine million people in Manila
    who have no gate, no yard, not even a house.
If only I could own something in the world,
    even if it were only a gate,
    even if it were messed up at election time.
Good night, madame, and you, too, sir.
Excuse me. I've got to keep working."

Cheap

I was waiting for Peter
    at the coffee shop of the Ptarmigan Inn.
The waitress had just poured my second cup of coffee,
    when two men sat down at the table next to me:

"July 1996! and last night was the first time
    that territorial government officials
    cared to ask us in Hay River
    about the best ways to cut costs."

"And you knew what to answer them:

    'Cut free housing for Indians,
    and you'll save millions of dollars.'"

"Darn right!
Indians shouldn't get anything for free."

"You know, I used to think like that.
Now, I feel the government is smart
    to give them their houses."

"No way! I work and I pay for everything I have.
Why give them everything free?"

"Cool off, Mike.
A few years back, I saw the map
    that showed Indians' trails and campsites
    all over that frozen land.
There was not one square mile
    without Indian footprints.
They said, 'This is our land.' It surely was."

"So what?"

"In those days, we couldn't cut a seismic line,
explore anywhere, start any mine,
without meeting Indians in the bush.
Then, the territorial government
moved to Yellowknife in 1967.
The new Commissioner, Raw Power Hodgson,
figured out how to get Indians out of the bush.
He promised them everything they wanted
if they moved into villages and towns."

"Now, we're stuck with his promises."

"But it worked.
Finance guys, mining outfits and oil companies
wanted to go full speed ahead with exploration.
They needed roads, airstrips, the whole thing.
Once the Indians were parked in villages,
they didn't care much about their land any more,
and the whole country became ours."

"Nobody forced them Indians to move.
They wanted all the luxuries we have,
beer, bingos, T.V., and video games.
If that's what they want, fine,
but we shouldn't have to pay for it."

"But if they can't afford to live in town,
they'll return to the bush and occupy their land again."

"O.K.! Give them small shacks, that's all.
Some of their houses are better than mine."

"On the other hand,
if we give them houses full of gadgets,
complex controls and electronic stuff
which they cannot repair themselves,
it makes them more dependent on us.
Makes them feel like a bunch of know-nothings.
Now, they'll never have the guts
to stand up for their land."

"Well, let them have houses, but no free services,
    no free water, firewood or heating oil."

"Mike, when I came to Hay River in 1962,
    I watched them Indians work.
They got everything from the land:
    water, wood, meat, fish, berries,
    logs for their houses, plants for medicine.
They used to love the land like their mother.
You see, they lived quietly in the bush,
    they learned from the trees and the animals.
    They had time to think, to figure things out.
    They built up strong minds and strong spirits."

"Now, all I see is a bunch of lazybones
    sitting in armchairs,
    drinking, and watching Hockey Night in Canada."

"But that's what I mean, Mike.
With free housing
    they've lost their connection to the land.
Now, their minds are already too weak
    to oppose anything we want to do in that country."

"But they don't even thank the government
    or me and you who pay taxes."

"But Mike, we've got their land.
    The whole land is now free for private use,
    dams, roads, mines, exploitation."

"I guess it makes sense after all.
Housing and feeding a few thousand Indians,
    in return for one million square kilometres!"

"You bet it's pretty cheap!"

Bridge

A meeting in Yellowknife gathered Dene and whites
    coming from a variety of races,
    religions, political and economic systems.

Members of the dominant society
    were preaching accommodation
    to those who have already been
    so accommodating for two hundred years:

> "We can all meet halfway ..."
>
> "We want to find a middle ground ..."
>
> "We must all compromise at the centre ..."
>
> "It's easy to start from a midway location ..."
>
> "There's always a golden mean position ..."

Not new ideas for Benitra, a Dene elder:

> "We've walked halfway long time ago,
>   and halfway again,
>   and halfway many more times.
>
> Now, I have a question for you:
>
>   Have you ever heard
>   of anybody building a bridge
>   by starting at the centre?"

Bliss

"Camillo, do you remember we used to

sing to the sunrise and to the sunset,
bask in the sun's sensual embrace,
ask the rain to soak and cleanse us,
forget about time while gazing at the moon,
ask the clouds to build new dreams for us?"

"Yes, and I recall our bliss when

we allowed total darkness to hold us,
we printed our hands on frosted windows,
we let a stream rush through our fingers,
we contemplated snowdrifts sculptured by the wind."

"What a joy it was to

listen to the trees,
pick up wild raspberries,
glorify fireweed and water lilies,
caress a rock or the bark of a tree,
climb a high hill just for nothing."

"How often did we

honour moose and caribou,
watch migrating birds,
discover evasive ptarmigans,
laugh at the ravens' antics,
crawl very close to a rabbit!"

"I wish we could do that again!"

"Why don't we?"

Bible and Gun

At the Winnipeg airport,
    I crawled towards the security check.
Ten feet ahead of me,
    a man carried a Gospel book,
    a large volume with intricate designs on the cover.
The man and the book were waved through.

But for the next man, the scanner shrilled fearfully.
Two policemen appeared out of nowhere,
    found a small revolver on the would-be passenger,
    and whisked off the protesting man:

        "I know what I'm doing,
        I won't use it, I swear I won't use it,
        I would never use a revolver in a plane.
        I don't even have a single bullet with me."

He was dragged away,
    and I am sure that he missed his flight.

If a gunman started to shoot during a flight,
    what's the worst that could happen?
A plane crash, one hundred people killed,
    endless investigations and costly lawsuits.
But thousands of planes would still fly safely,
    economies flourish,
    governments keep control,
    and millions of people enjoy their lives.

Now, suppose that one man with the Gospel
    would have faith in Jesus' message
    and teach dozens, thousands, millions of people:

"If you are a master, act as a servant."

"Give to everyone who asks,
give up everything you have."

"When someone asks you for something, give it to them."

"When you prepare a good meal,
don't invite those who can invite you back,
but only the poor and the crippled, the blind and the lame."

What if dozens, thousands and millions of people
decided to live according to Jesus' message?

Our financial institutions would crumble.
How could our economy survive
without greed and competition?

Our political structures would tumble.
Can a country be ruled on love?
without confrontation?
without an official opposition?

Our social system would melt away.
What is there to do
if there are no ladders to climb?
no useless wants to fulfill?
no neighbours to impress?

Any page of the Gospel could destroy our society
much faster than a thousand guns.

But, if a man carries a gun, we assume he will use it;
if a man carries a Gospel book, we assume he won't.

Wolf Pups

In the 1950s and 1960s,
the government forced or bribed a lot of Dene
into moving into larger towns or cities:

"There we will give you better services."

In fact, the government
wanted the ancestral lands of the Dene
to be available for mining and industry.

Andrew, a Chipewyan Dene one year younger than me,
lived on the Southern shore of Tunedhe (Great Slave Lake),
in the small village of Rocher River.
Andrew and his friends
gave up their prosperous self-governing community,
and a district rich in meat, fish and fur.
They moved to Yellowknife, where aboriginal people
were expected to forget who they were and become 'white.'

Andrew lived on the fringe and worked now and then,
until he was crippled in an accident
and hence needed a crutch to walk.
He stayed with his blind mother
until she died in May 1974, at the age of 75.
He inherited her small shack:
one wood stove, one bed, one water barrel.
In the late 1970s, while gone for a few days,
Andrew let somebody stay in his house.

The house burned down.

Andrew couldn't rebuild because city regulations
demanded the disappearance of small houses
and their replacement by sumptuous residences.
So Andrew slept here and there, or at the Salvation Army.
Two or three times a week, he joined me for breakfast,
and he enchanted me with his stories.

One night in June 1989,
    Andrew was out with a few friends.
He was stabbed in the leg, lost a lot of blood,
    was sent to an Edmonton hospital and died,
    a victim of what politicians and business people call
    "the negative impacts of development."

And now, here is one of Andrew's breakfast stories:

> "Ten years ago, my friend Baptist and I
>   were hunting in the Barren Land,
>   and we discovered five wolf pups in a den.
>
> "I had always dreamed
>   of using fast wolves to pull my toboggan.
> My dream was coming true.
>
> "Even if I took good care of them,
>   for a while the pups seemed to lose weight.
> But rapidly they started to fill out again,
>   their bodies and legs stretching long and strong,
>   all taller than the best dogs I ever had.
> That team would be my fastest!
> My friends came to admire my pups,
>   and I felt they were kind of jealous of me.
>
> "I bought a new set of harness—
>   and I mean, of first quality leather.
> The first time I put the pups in the harness,
>   they jumped wildly, as all pups do.
> I talked to them nicely,
>   and I even caressed them,
>   something I had done to no dog before.
> Slowly they got used to pulling the toboggan,
>   and their strong muscles sped me away.
>
> "Every evening, when we stopped in the bush,
>   I cut spruce boughs for them to sleep on;
> I fed them the best fish I caught,
>   and caribou meat in times of plenty.
> A few times, when we were short of food,
>   I fed them what was to have been my supper.

"When they were one year old, I drove them to the Barren Land
to set a few traps, and to shoot a few caribou.
On the third day, I put them in the harness,
as I had done dozens of times.
One started to pull right and left,
and soon the five were jumping all over.
Before I could even think what to do,
one had chewed off his harness.
All—in a flash—did the same, dashed away,
and disappeared beyond a hill.

"I knew this land, and I could make it home on my own,
but I felt so sorry for my five friends.

"'Nobody will feed them at the proper time.
Now, they need to roam all over in search of food,
and they will go hungry at times
in their desolate world.

"'Nobody will caress them, care for them,
and tell them encouraging words.
Now they must rely only on themselves,
and face cruel winters and blizzards.

"'What a disaster for such animals
previously treated so well and loved so much.'

"The longer I walked,
the sorrier I felt for them ...

until, the second day, I stopped on the trail,
and shook my head:

'But, anyway, now they are free.'"

Witness

On a Friday, I visited the Dene National office,
and someone told me:

"Next week, there is a leadership meeting
in Tets'ehxe Tú (Drum Lake)."

On Sunday, a chief asked me:

"Did you hear about the Tets'ehxe Tú meeting?"

On Monday, another Dene informed me:

"The charter plane to Tets'ehxe Tú leaves
tomorrow at 9 a.m."

Traditional Dene don't ask questions
which can be answered by yes or no.
It helps to avoid awkward situations:

"If one expects a 'yes' answer,
she may feel bad to hear a 'no.'
One may like to answer 'no,'
but he says 'yes' to please the questioner."

Guessing from the information I received,
I went to the airport on Tuesday morning,
and there was a seat for me on the plane.

Tets'ehxe Tú has been the traditional home
of the Shíhta Got'įne (Mountain People),
known for their song-making and dances,
and well respected for their medicine powers.
They are famous for the invention and use
of the fifteen-metre-long moose skin boat.

Under the radiant sun of July, 1979,
Tets'ehxe Tú sparkles as a jewel.

On the first day of the meeting,
I sit in a corner and I listen,
and on the second day, and on the third day.
Then, in the evening, I meet one leader:

"I had the feeling that I was invited here.
Am I expected to do something?"

He smiles kindly, and he walks away.
Later on, another Dene is a bit more helpful:

"René, you are witnessing our discussions,
listening to our plans for the future
of our nation and of our children.
We didn't ask you for anything,
so you may simply rejoice
to share our vision and our hopes."

Wisdom

In November 1990,
I happened to visit the Rainbow Lake oil field,
and the Zama school.
The children were seven or eight years old,
and a catechist talked about belonging:

"Who do you belong to?"

"Mom and dad."

"Who else do you belong to?"

"We belong to the earth!"

We truly need schools,
so that children
can teach adults.

Tug-O-War

In 1521, Magellan 'discovered' a cluster of islands
which he named Philippines after Philip II, king of Spain.
The Spaniards settled on a few islands,
and made sporadic, always futile, attempts
to control the northern tribes and their mountain range.
Yet, they baptized it 'Cordillera' or 'Nueva Castilla,'
and labelled its inhabitants 'Ygorotes gentiles,' pagan Igorots.

In 1898, the U.S.A. defeated the Spanish fleet at Manila
and later claimed the Philippines as its colony.
The U.S. Bureau of Non-Christian Tribes
promoted the gradual assimilation of the Igorots,
now branded as one of the 'cultural minorities.'

After white people invade ancestral territories,
destroy 'ethnic' cultures, condemn 'savage' rites,
and oppress aboriginal nations into powerlessness,
they like to promote indigenous research and studies.
In 1904, one hundred and fourteen Igorots and Tinguians
were exhibited during the Saint Louis Exposition in the U.S.A.
Some Igorots were displayed in England
as "rare specimens of savage people."

In 1904, Bontoc was named the capital of the Mountain Province
and its marvellous modern museum displays early photographs
glorifying Governor John Evans, his officials,
and their two-storey government building
overlooking the thatched-roof huts of the Igorots.
Other photographs artistically present
the traditional lifestyle and practices
of the Bontoc, Kalinga, and Ifugao tribes.

In a 1909 photograph,
    a tug-o-war opposes eight Talubin Bontocs to eight Samoki Bontocs.
Short and stocky, all wear only G-strings and head purses.
Their skin is as brown as the earth they are digging their heels in.
Every fibre of every muscle of every tilted man
    is strained past a reasonable limit.
A superhuman energy on one side
    matches a superhuman energy on the other side,
    and the power of the earth beneath them
    may prevent either side from ever budging.
Will brothers keep on fighting brothers for ever?

However, the Bontocs on both sides
    may all be on the losing side.
Behind them stands a team of eight U.S. officials
    wearing white hats, white shirts,
    white jackets, white pants and black ties.
Some encourage their favourite team with hand signs.
    Others stand cool, tall and straight,
    obviously anxious to declare winners and losers.

A caption explains:

> "The U.S. Secretary of the Interior of the Philippine Islands
>   introduced the games to divert the people from head hunting."

But I overheard the comments of a visiting couple:

> "Ben, did U.S. people use Igorots
>   to celebrate their Fourth of July,
>   as British used Nigerians
>   to celebrate their Queen's birthday?"

> "My dear, isn't the first goal of any colonizer
>   to keep the colonized busy with trifles,
>   with no time to reflect on their true situation?
> As long as colonized people fight each other
>   how can they unite against their common enemy?"

At least, that's the way it was long, long ago.

Terrorism

"Kevin, *The Globe and Mail* reads:
'The G7 countries
vowed to redouble their efforts to fight terrorism.'
Have you seen it?"

"No. When was that?"

"In yesterday's paper, July 31, 1996.
I guess those are the seven rich countries:
U.S.A., England, France, Japan, Canada, Italy and Germany.
The paper adds:

'They decided to push forward
a 25-point program to eliminate terrorism.'"

"Does it mean that the G7 will stop
the World Bank and the International Monetary Fund
from terrorizing poor countries
into accepting fraudulent loans
and unjust economic policies
which benefit only the rich countries?"

"The U.S. Attorney General, Janet Reno,
admitted that 'terrorism takes many forms.'"

"Have the seven richest countries promised
never again to terrorize any other country
whose political ideology they don't like?"

"They only talked about terrorism."

"Have the G7 decided
to stop terrorizing the world's aboriginal nations
out of their ancestral lands, cultures and resources?"

"The British Home Secretary, Michael Howard, said,
'We cannot offer our citizens total protection,
but that reinforces the imperative for us
to do everything we can.'"

"Every hour, 500 people die
from imposed hunger or hunger-related illnesses.
Will the five hundred corporations
which control 25% of the world's economic output
stop terrorizing millions of people into starvation
in order to feed their own greed?"

"The way that the paper explains it,
terrorism is much worse than all that.
It's like when, a few days ago, two U.S. citizens
died from a bomb explosion
during the Olympics in Atlanta."

The Loop

November 1953, 25 degrees below zero Centigrade,
small lakes and rivers are frozen solid.
I have been five months in Rádęlį Kǫ́ (Fort Good Hope).
Most of the Dene have left the village,
and are scattered over thousands of square kilometres
for the trapping and hunting season.

A Dene arrives from Tuk'á Kénílįne (Loon River)
which empties into Dehcho (Mackenzie River),
forty kilometres downstream from the village.

"George is very, very sick."

It means that a priest should go there
to give him the Last Rites,
the church's special prayer for the sick and the dying.

Since the first snowfall in September,
I have trained myself as a dog musher
by driving the mission's five dogs
in the vicinity of the village:

"Now, I have to travel on my own,
my first priestly ministry by dogteam!
At least, I cannot get lost,
I only need to follow the Dehcho River bank."

Five kilometres from Rádęlį Kó,
I face the frozen Xayįts'á Nilįné (Hare River).
However, heavy snowfalls have cracked the ice,
and the overflow water is 10 centimetres deep.
I stand on the toboggan
and I gently encourage the dogs to go ahead.
Probably desirous to test a new driver,
they refuse to wade into the water.

No manual has taught me about such a situation.

"I will not turn back,
and I won't wet my only pair of moccasins."

Only one alternative is left.
I take off my moccasins and my socks,
and I walk in the water across the river,
pulling the dogs behind me.

The rest of the trip goes more or less uneventfully.
I zigzag on the river among huge blocks of ice
piled up by the fall winds and the river current.
Or I drive along the steep river bank,
continuously straining
to prevent the toboggan from sliding down.
Any Dene who saw my tracks later on
must have had a good laugh.

Daylight is short at the Arctic Circle in October,
and I feel proud that, even in darkness,
I easily reach the Dene camp on top of the bank.
A family occupies a log building,
and I wonder why another cabin is left vacant
while George and his parents live in a nearby tent.

The canvas tent measures about three metres by four.
Outside, at its front and back,
two spruce poles tied into an X
support the extremities of a long pole
which runs lengthwise under the canvas roof
and exits at both ends.

A thick layer of spruce bows provides a soft floor.
George is lying in his sleeping bag,
under the top pole, at the back of the tent.
Right over his head, at the end of a thirty-centimetre string,
hangs a loop, probably made from a willow branch.

The loop is so perfectly handmade
    that I can't see where the ends fit together.
In my former country, I have never seen such a loop,
    and I am intrigued and suspicious,
    as one is often afraid of the unknown.
Is it a superstition, a Dene magic rite?
How can it fit with my own prayers?

The Dene themselves probably wonder
    if my own prayers are a kind of magic.
I pray in Latin, the only language God understands,
    and the book, the oil and the religious garb I wear
    are imported from thousands of kilometres away.

The next morning, Antoine, George's father,
    visits his fishnet set under the river ice.
The net has collected a lot of dirt,
    and Antoine brings it back to clean it.
After most of the water has dripped off the net,
    Antoine slides the suspicious loop along the top pole
    towards the front of the tent,
    where the net lies in a tub.
He grabs one end of the fishnet,
    slides it through the loop,
    and, sitting on the floor,
    he pulls the fishnet a little at a time,
    and shakes and cleans the dirt away.

Split!

Délı̨ne (Fort Franklin) is a cold and windy place.
Every winter, we needed cords and cords of firewood
to heat the church and the mission residence.

Every day of winter,
the Dene used to hitch their dogs,
go to the nearby bush and cut the firewood
they needed for that night and the next day.
Not being a Dene, I preferred
to cut my yearly supply at once, and to store it.

Fall was the best time to cut firewood;
mosquitoes had disappeared,
the ground was frozen, with little snow.
My five dogs hauled the firewood to the mission yard,
four or five trips for one cord.

A small engine and a circular saw made it easy
to cut the wood into required lengths.
Later on, in winter, the wood blocks were split,
easy work in really cold weather.

For two days, Peter had been splitting wood blocks
in the yard behind the mission building.
In the afternoon, three Dene were visiting me,
and, about 2 o'clock, I sent a young boy
to invite him for a cup of tea with us all.

"Peter, how is it going?"

"I've just finished it all."

"Wow, you worked so fast!"

I felt happy, we talked and drank tea,
    told stories and laughed for half an hour.
Then Peter looked at the fading light
    of that short winter day:

"Well, I better go and keep working."

"What work?"

"Well, splitting all that wood."

"But you told me you had split it all."

"Yes."

"So, is it all split or not?"

"Nobody could have finished that work already!"

"Then, why did you tell me it was all done?"

"Well, I made you happy for half an hour, didn't I?"

The Secret

"Father, I need your advice and your help.
I am a young priest, and you're an old one.
Father, women look so attractive, so desirable.
Their gestures are so graceful.
Their feelings seem to run so deep.
Their thinking contrasts so much with ours.
Father, women disturb my peace of mind.
Is there a way I can get rid of those longings?"

"Oh yes, there's a way, an easy one.
If you're interested, I'll tell you the secret.
Then, you will view women as cold as statues,
    their eyes as lifeless as old pieces of glass,
    and their gestures as if performed by robots.
Women's ideas will appear to be senseless
    and their feelings totally shallow.
I can tell you the secret right now."

"Does that secret work every time?"

"Yes, as soon as someone hears the words."

"I mean ... Are you sure it will work for me?"

"I guarantee it will work."

"Well, thank you, Father.
I'll call on you again, for sure very soon."

I remember every word of that conversation
    but I have forgotten
    if I was the young priest or the old one.

Culture Shock

After living four months in the Philippines,
    and taking a thirteen-hour flight from Manila,
    I landed in Vancouver on a late afternoon in May.
I dropped my suitcase at the Oblate house,
    at the corner of Maple and Arbutus,
    and, by 8 p.m., I had walked around a dozen blocks.

All streets were empty, even empty of garbage.

Houses were built from real building material.
All stood behind green lawns, away from the street,
not a poster on the walls,
    not a door open onto the street.

A dozen cars glided silently by,
    without dragging a cloud of smoke behind.
One car was parked in front of every house,
    but no tricycles, no colourful jeepneys.

I didn't see one child outside.
I met only two people on the sidewalk,
    one a man fatter than any I had seen in months.

On the sidewalks, nobody was cooking,
    eating, or fixing a car engine;
Nobody selling peanuts, chewing gum,
    or smoking cigarettes one at a time.

I pinched myself:
    Had I landed in a deserted town?

Sharing

In a dentist's waiting room in Edmonton,
Lucille glanced through the magazine *Up Here,*
published in Yellowknife, N.W.T.,
to lure tourists "up north."

People who learn geography from maps go "up north."
Dene, who live with their land and rivers,
go "down north," because most rivers flow northward.

The advertising worked on Lucille.
One month later, she boarded the Greyhound bus
for a twenty-two-hour ride to Yellowknife.
In Enterprise, south of Great Slave Lake,
she transferred to the Arctic Frontier Coach,
and she noticed a young couple who looked Indian.

"Where are you from?"

"We are Dene from Bèchokǫ̀.
White people call it Fort Rae.
We belong to the Dogrib Nation.
Our community is the best of all."

"If I stop in your village,
is there a hotel where I could stay?"

"There is no hotel, and you don't need one.
You can stay at our home."

"You won't charge me anything?"

"We never charge anybody.
We share everything,
among ourselves and with strangers too.
That's the Dene way."

Lucille visited Bèchokǫ̀, the church, the school,
the store, the tribal office and the old folks' home.
From Pat, Richard, Adele, Gordon and Lena,
she learned more about the Dene way:

"Anybody who needs my truck can borrow it."

"When I am short of gas, my neighbours give me some."

"Sometimes I pay the electricity bill for my friends."

"When I catch a lot of fish,
I give fish to those who are not so lucky."

"If people are short of money for bingo,
I lend them whatever they need."

"If some people have no work and no income,
or if hungry children come to our house,
we feed them the best food we have."

"When someone dies, we all share the funeral expenses."

Lucille was impressed:

"When B.H.P. extracts diamonds from Dogrib land,
it will pay you royalties every year,
probably millions of dollars.
Will you share that money with the other Indians
who don't have diamonds on their land?"

"No way!"

Shackles

One of those long winter nights
    when the best thing to do is to sit around the stove,
Grandpa Angus was ready with another story.
"It happened in the early 1930's, before I was born
    and I heard it from Sam Norn himself.

"Everybody was dancing heartily in Alec Loutit's Hall.
    Jim Lafferty was calling the dances,
        the best ever caller in Denınu (Fort Resolution).
    The dance over, everyone walked out,
        still cheerful and enchanted.

"Nobody seemed to know why or how it happened,
    but outside, Jim Lafferty slapped Jimmy Donovan,
    a white trapper from Rat River.
    Vic Lafferty, Fred Beaulieu, Edward Balsillie,
        James Fabian, and Albert Norn were standing nearby,
        but there was no fight at all, so nobody interfered.

"Jimmy Donovan complained to the R.C.M.P.
A white man who beat an Indian was never charged,
    but Jim Lafferty was sentenced
    to six months hard labour.
    The other five men got three months each.

    "'Me too,' Sam told me,
    'I stood outside after the dance.
    My eyesight was already poor,
    and I couldn't work too hard;
    may be that's why the R.C.M.P. let me go.'

"You know Sam; now he's totally blind.

"The six prisoners, two by two,
    were shackled by the ankles.

"It was winter,
but they slept on a grey blanket on the jail floor,
and in those days, floors were not insulated.
At night, if one wanted to go outside to pee,
the other man chained to him had to go also.

"At that time,
Harry Balsillie was the special constable.
Each month he was paid sixty dollars by cheque,
and sixty dollars worth of groceries.

"The police ordered Harry:

> 'We want to build a new barrack.
> Everyday you'll take the prisoners
> to cut logs near the Nagle Channel.
> Give them only hardtacks to eat
> and water to drink.
> If you make tea in the bush,
> it must be only for yourself.
> Do not give them tea or any other food,
> and, if you do, you'll lose your job.'

"But Harry's wife made sandwiches for the prisoners,
and Harry took a chance feeding them.
In the bush, they took turns eating:
one ate while the other five worked,
and Harry watched the trail
for any possible intruding police.

"Why did we allow such things to happen?"

Seventy-Two

In 1918, in Almonte, Ontario,
Fr. John Mary Fraser founded a missionary society
destined to minister exclusively in China
where he had served for the previous ten years.
Three years later, the society settled in Scarborough,
and it still shines as the "Scarboro Foreign Missions."
When political events locked the Chinese door
the Scarboros scattered into various other mission fields.

I celebrated Christmas 1982
with Charlie and Gary, two S.F.M's.,
at their San Fernando mission in the Philippines,
and I was blessed with one more of their stories:

"Scarboro Missionaries reached Japan in 1948.
In 1951, they built their first church in Aino,
and also served in many Kyushu Island parishes.
In those days, most Catholics believed
that outside their own Church there was no salvation.

"Japanese, influenced by the Confucian way of life,
organized their homogeneous society
around Buddhist temples and Shinto shrines.
Catholic missionaries fished
from a sea of Buddhism and Shintoism
one soul here and a few souls there,
but, after twenty-five years,
Catholics were still outnumbered 300 to one.

"At New Year's time,
every Japanese visits a Shinto shrine.
One such day, Fr. John Mary and Fr. Rogers,
standing in the Osaka Scarboro mission,
overlooked thousands of Buddhists in a square.

"Both priests probably also contemplated
their own beliefs, commitments, and dreams,
those which had borne fruit—and the others.
Calm and solemn, seventy-two-year-old Fr. John Mary
turned to his younger friend:

"'Come to think of it, I don't believe
that all those people will go to hell.'"

The honesty of that open-minded old man
overwhelmed me:

"What great truth will I myself discover
when I turn seventy-two?"

Savage Fight

In 1953, I sailed from Le Havre
  on the *Homeric,* a Greek ship with an all-Italian crew.
Even with a 24-hour storm,
  the passage to Quebec City was a five-day vacation,
  and, for me, an opportunity to learn my first English words.

From Quebec, I took the CN train westwards,
  and stopped in Montreal, Ottawa, Toronto, Winnipeg.
In Winnipeg I dared to open an English newspaper,
  and I was struck by a gigantic title spread over one page:

SAVAGE FIGHT BETWEEN BOMBERS AND ESKIMOS

"Savage" is similar to the French *sauvage*. I understood.
"Fight" I knew. I lived my teen-age years during WWII.
"Between": I had already learned that word.
"Bombers": During the war, the bombers
  were the toughest, trained for the worst.
"Eskimos": As a child in France,
  I knew about these short people
  dressed in furs and living in igloos
  where it is winter all year round.

Was I ever shocked!

"What does that dreadful title mean?
I always thought that all Canadians
  live in wealth, peace and harmony.
I had never heard of racial problems in Canada.
What happened?
Did the Eskimos rebel against the Canadian Government?
Who sent the Bombers to quash the revolt?
Where did that savage fight take place?
How many hundreds of people were killed?
And ... why am I coming to such a country?"

Anxiously, I looked at the first column of text.
On the first line, I didn't understand a word,
nor on the second line.
But on the third line I read: "football,"
a word I had known since I was a baby.
I burst out laughing.

"That's it.
Bombers and Eskimos must be two football teams
who fought a savage game.
Then, I don't have to worry:
Canada must still be a safe, pleasant place."

Salvation

"Knock ... Knock ... Knock ..."

I was visiting Arturo,
when he went to open the front door.
From the kitchen, I overheard:

"Good morning, sir."

"Good morning, sir."

"Are you saved?"

"I don't know."

"You need to know."

"I don't care."

"You need to care."

"Maybe."

"Take this booklet, and you'll find out."

"No, thanks."

"But you need to be saved."

"There's plenty of time."

"Do you know about Jesus?"

"He's a good guy."

"Do you know about his Gospel?"

"A little bit."

"Like what?"

"One day he was preaching.
People were not interested,
and they left him.
He respected them and he let them go.
He was not pushy."

"Yes, I know that story.
Chapter 6, verse 66 in John's gospel.
Now, let's talk about your salvation."

Reconciliation

Liane closed her *Maclean's* magazine:

"You know, June, the world has changed a lot in 1988.
Everybody is getting friendly."

"Yes, Mikhail Gorbachev was welcomed in New York.
I saw a photo of him and Reagan smiling at each other."

"Yasser Arafat spoke at the United Nations.
He had a 'constructive discussion' with U.S. Secretary,
George Schultz."

"France, Germany, England, haven't fought for forty years,
and European nations are planning a United Parliament."

"China and the U.S.S.R. are talking to each other,
and also Vietnam and Kampuchea."

"Inuit of all countries formed the Circumpolar Conference.
Seven people from U.S.S.R. and four from Canada
skied the Polar Bridge together."

"Iran and Iraq agreed to a cease-fire.
South Korea and North Korea started 'high level talks.'"

"South African and Cuban soldiers are leaving Namibia.
In May, Soviet troops began withdrawing from Afghanistan."

"The Nobel Peace Prize went to the U.N. peacekeeping force—
10,000 men from 35 nations united for peace,
of whom 1,300 Canadians."

"By the way, June,
how did you make out with Betty last week?"

"Don't mention Betty!
I don't want to hear from her,
to talk about her,
to have anything to do with her."

Recession

On March 9, 1991, I was flying from Edmonton to Vancouver,
  and dozing off when the attendant passed the newspapers.
The passenger on my right picked up a *Globe and Mail,*
  and, once coffee had been served, he shared the news with me.

"Bad news! Jobless rate hits 10.2 per cent,
  the worst in more than five years."

"What a frustrating feeling for workers
  suddenly unable to bring home a paycheque!"

"They'll have to learn about market forces,
  the global recession, international trends."

"But how can one explain that to hungry children?"

"And look, down the page, there's even much worse:

'MacMillan Bloedel executives suffered deep cuts:
Executive vice-president Don McLauchlin's salary
  dropped from $412,800 to $240,000.
John Ross dropped from $456,434 to $213,105.
Ray Smith went down from $625,000 to only $350,000.'"

"That's significant, but, I don't think
  they or their children will go hungry."

"But salary cuts are more dramatic for executives.
Ordinary workers are used to shrinking salaries.
A little more, a little less,
  they've learned to manage with little.
But executives are used to luxury, to comfort,
  to gratification, to eccentricity.
They just cannot learn to live otherwise."

Quarter

For one week in November,
Łútsel K'e (Snowdrift) organized sessions and workshops,
games and dances, picnics and elaborate meals
to celebrate the many people
who had become sober in the past ten years.
Even the clouds joined in our festivities
and provided relatively mild weather.

For the Saturday evening potluck supper,
everyone gathered at the community hall.
Babies slept on benches, children played all over,
elders and youngsters chatted joyfully.

Awards were presented
to those who had regained control of their lives.
All speeches stirred deep feelings in me,
and none was too long.

After the meal, one hundred people
formed a giant circle for a last thanksgiving.
As I held August's hand on one side,
and Gina's hand on the other,
a four-year-old boy squeezed in next to me.
Twice my fingers searched for his hand
but he offered me only his fist,
a fist tight to the end,
a fist holding a quarter.

So little, so much!

Goldfish

I was a small boy in a small town.
One day, on my way home from school,
    I noticed that a house was vacant.
The door was ajar, and I walked in
    like an explorer in an unknown country.

What a dismal place!
No furniture left,
    garbage here and there,
    and a doll sleeping on dirty rags.
I was ready to walk out
    when I noticed a goldfish
    swimming in a glass bowl.

I had always wanted a goldfish,
    but I decided against bringing it home.

The next morning I was unusually anxious
    about going to school.
The goldfish was still there!
I knelt down, looked, and wondered
    at the pretty fish, so full of life.
I slid the bowl into the sunshine,
    and the fish became transparent.
I liked it so much.

How could they forget such a lovely fish?
Had they lost all their humanity?
I didn't know such big words as "criminal negligence"
    but I knew that's what it was.
I was also thankful for their carelessness:
Now this was my fish!

I didn't tell my parents or my friends:
    the goldfish remained my dear secret.
Each day, on my way to school and back,

I watched my fish swimming swiftly
up and down and all around.
I told it how graceful it was,
and it seemed to like it.

Other people also must have gone into the house:
More garbage, more broken windows,
and more dust in the fishbowl.

One morning, my fish was lying down
and I had to shake the bowl
to bring it back to life.
Then, it was swimming kind of slow,
and, even in the bright sunshine,
its skin looked rather dull.

In the afternoon, I started to panic:
my fish was going to die!
What could I do?
All I knew about fish was to admire them.

I could have asked for help,
but that meant sharing my secret.
I prayed very hard:
If God had created all the fish,
She had to care for my fish.

My friend John owned a bird in a cage,
so he was a specialist about animals.
After he promised "Cross my heart,"
that he wouldn't tell my secret,
I took him to the dying fish.

Nothing was a problem for John,
not even such a desperate situation:

"That's easy!
Your fish needs more than your love.
Throw away that stinking water,
and fill up the bowl with fresh water."

Primitive

Tannis had been lured from Calgary to Sahtú (Great Bear Lake)
by the fish stories of a co-worker.
Now, day after day, his own catches
surpassed the stories he had been told.
He was also catching wonderful stories,
legends and traditions from his guide.

"Joe, you told me that for centuries
the Dene had no school,
no police, no jail, no court system,
no daycare centre, no old folks' home,
no welfare agent, no parliament, no election,
... and that your nation survived
for ten thousand years."

"It's true, maybe even for longer."

"How could you survive for so long?"

"Simply because we had no school,
no police, no jail, no court system,
no daycare centre, no old folks' home,
no welfare agent, no parliament, no election."

Pressing Needs

In Rádęlı̨ Kǫ́ (Fort Good Hope),
    Kotse's cabin overlooked Jackfish Creek.
The whitewashed logs, precisely dovetailed,
    sparkled under the brilliant May sunshine.
Through the open door, sun rays danced on the floor boards
    whipsawed and handplaned years ago.

A blackened tea kettle crowned the stove
    chiselled out of a 45-gallon oil drum,
    and as unique as its maker.
Some china decorated the three shelves.
A fish net, through a loop, hung from a beam.
In a corner, lay the tools of a hunter-trapper-fisherman.

Kotse had been a widower for three years.
He sat at the table, on a simple bench,
    eating a piece of whitefish with his fingers.
He had forks,
    but fish from one's fingers tastes so much better.

A man's shadow appeared on the floor,
    followed by a man in a three-piece suit and shiny shoes,
    himself followed by a Dene interpreter.
The man from another town, or from another world, explained:

"I am running in the next election,
    and, if you and your friends vote for me,
    I can get you anything you want."

"Really?"

"Really! My researcher has advised me that
all you people here have a strong urge
to better your lot,
to lead a more rewarding life,
and to enrich your personalities.
Once you make me aware of your pressing needs,
I will procure for you whatever you need."

"For sure?"

"For sure!"

"Anything?"

"Anything!"

"Well, I'll be frank with you.
Could you get me a bit of salt
to sprinkle over my fish?"

Olympics

From February 2 to 8, 1997,
Toronto and Collingwood
hosted the “Special Winter Olympics.”
Seventy-two countries sent 2,000 athletes,
ranging from 8 to 66 years,
all with mental handicaps.

The Special Olympics, founded in 1968 in Chicago,
are held every two years,
less concerned about winning or losing,
than about participation.

Few rich countries pay attention;
an individual medal tally is not kept,
and national anthems are not played.

Business cares little for that kind of sports:
the 1997 budget was only $9.4 million,
and not one of the athletes was for sale.

A Canadian stood on the podium
to receive his second gold medal in downhill skiing.
He turned to his U.S. friend who had placed second:

“I’ve got one gold medal already,
but no silver medal.
You don’t have a gold medal yet,
can we trade?”

‘Retarded’ people?

Growing Down

Pope John Paul II
has been loved by many and criticized by many,
but his photograph adorns every R.C. building.

In 1992, I stayed in Łútsel K'e (Snowdrift) for a few days
and I resided at the Mission building.

As usual, people visited me
to chat, to drink tea, to tell stories,
or, as they say, "for nothing."
One afternoon, I was talking with a Dene woman,
while her little boy inspected the building.
For a while, he looked up the wall
at a photograph of the pope.
Then he looked at me.
Again at the photograph.
Again at me:

"Is that you when you were older?"

Oh's and Ah's!

On Christmas Day, I visited a few homes,
tasted fancy food, laughed with friends,
and shared in the community spirit.
An old bachelor appreciates such treats.

Ask children what Christmas is about,
and many will answer: "Toys."
I have no children or grandchildren to buy toys for,
but modern toys intrigue me
with their complexity, their unreal shapes,
their array of colours, and their price tags.
I was born long before plastic was invented.

Boxing Day was over, but toys and boxes
still decorated many floors.

A "Great Adventure Pirate Ship"
lay on its side, grounded behind a coach.
The pirates themselves, grounded on cushions,
were watching a cartoon about elephants.

A $119.99 Indy Pedal Car
"with turbo shift and ratcheting sound"
had overturned and waited for a tow truck.
The driver lay nearby, not injured, but sound asleep.

An $89.99 "L'il Kawasaki ATV,"
and a $99.99 "Radio-controlled Cyclone Truck,"
had seemingly reached their range limit.

A $24.99 Harley Davidson motorcycle
had driven to the wall a $79.99 Rebel Wrecker.

A Barbie Doll "all set to dazzle"
lay under an Electronic Batmobile.

Only one toy reminded me of my own childhood:
    a train set with its locomotive, tender and cars.

Some children were watching TV,
    others, bored, turned in circles,
    their faces as dull as the dark clouds outside.
Maybe next Christmas will bring real excitement?

On my way home, I stopped at Isadore's house.
    For one hour, we enjoyed tea and cake,
    a few jokes and the usual teasing.
Off and on, I watched Kim, Jerry and Elora
    playing by themselves on the floor.
Their young imagination, totally free,
    kept inventing new games and new rules.
They laughed and shouted "Oh!" and "Ah!"
    at their achievements and frustrations,
    deeply enthused with the wooden blocks
    their parents had cut and painted for them.

Oh, Clock

Jolo

In January 1983, I happened
to visit the town of Jolo in the Philippines.
Another Oblate, Father Dorot,
invited me to his Siasi mission
where he was returning the next day.

Somebody had already explained to me:

"The Philippines is made up of 7,100 islands,
and every one of those islands
is surrounded by the sea."

So I expected to sail to another island
on one of those thousands of small boats
usually overloaded with freight and passengers.
In the evening I inquired:

"When does the boat sail from the harbour?"

"At 8:00 in the morning."

"How far is it from here to the harbour?"

"A twenty-minute walk."

"At what time will we leave from the house?"

"Oh, about 8:30."

We did, and we had a pleasant boat trip.

Kabacan

In the Philippines, private cars are rare,
  but thousands of buses crisscross the country
  on the few highways and on the many gravel roads.
There is no maximum seating capacity,
  and passengers may sit on the roof,
  or hang out from the windows.

In January 1983, fighting erupted now and then
  between the New People's Army and Marcos' army.
Most buses, afraid of unsafe roads,
  didn't travel after darkness
  which falls regularly at 6 p.m. all year round.

After a few days in Davao City,
  I boarded a bus to Kabacan
  to visit an Oblate priest there.
Arriving in Kabacan, I walked to the bus office:

"Tomorrow, at what time do buses leave
  from here to Cotabato City?"

"Every hour on the hour, from 5 a.m. to 5 p.m."

The next day, I showed up at about 4:45 p.m.
I waited for over half an hour,
  and then walked to one of the bus line staff:

"Yesterday, I was told
  a bus would leave at 5 p.m. to Cotabato City."

"The five o'clock? It was very early today, it's gone."

"That was the last bus today,
  so I have to wait till tomorrow?"

"I guess so."

The agent walked away ... but then turned back:

"No, you can go today,
because the four o'clock bus hasn't arrived yet.
It's very, very late; you can catch that one."

Yellowknife

Eight people were already present
and ready to start the meeting.

"Where is Peter?"

"Peter said he'd be here at nine o'clock.
Right now, it's 9:30,
so, he'll be here soon,
unless he's late."

Nice

In a nice church
with nice candles
and nice flowers
on a nice altar
a nice priest
in nice vestments
read a nice gospel
and said a nice mass
for nice people
nicely dressed
sitting in nice pews
who said nice prayers
to a nice Jesus
who had a nice birth
a nice life
a nice death
a nice resurrection
and now sits nicely
in a nice heaven
with his nice Father.

It was so nice!

New Baby

We want a baby.

We want a baby,
but it must be a boy.

We want a baby,
if the pregnancy
doesn't inconvenience us.

We want a baby,
if we don't have
to alter anything in our house.

We want a baby
exactly as tall as I am,
and with eyes like yours.

We want a baby
who must swim as fast as I
and sing as well as you.

We want a baby
if he has our own tastes,
and appreciates only what we like.

We want a baby who will
follow our own rules,
learn only what we know,
and believe only what is dear to us.

Oh yes,
we want a new church.

Mothers

In my book *Here I Sit* I explained
why in 1970 we celebrated
the centennial year of the N.W.T.
"We" included Queen Elizabeth, Prince Philip,
Prince Charles and Princess Anne.

You know how rigid is the Queen's timetable.
The program for July 8th indicated:

4:45 p.m.	Arrive Petitot Park.
5:00 p.m.	The Queen starts the Queen's Message relay for the opening of the Commonwealth Games.
5:10 p.m.	Depart Petitot Park.
5:15-5:35	(Reserved).
7:35 p.m.	Depart Fraser Tower Royal Apartments by car.

At 5:10 p.m., the Queen is ready to depart Petitot Park:

"Now, I will drive to Rainbow Valley
with only Prince Philip and the chauffeur.
No media will be allowed there.
After we cross to the island,
the R.C.M.P. will close the bridge."

Officials present on the sidewalk
started to pull their hair
and screamed silently inside:

"How does the Queen know about Rainbow Valley?"
"What can be of interest to her over there?"
"Why does she want to see those Indians?"

Rainbow Valley (Ndılon) is Yellowknife's Indian district.
In the 1950s, the white population
was getting too crowded in the Old Town,
and down on the Flats near the lakeshore.

So the New Town was built
further south, on top of the hill.
Indians had been around for centuries
and scattered their small shacks here and there.
They were moved three kilometres
to a valley at the end of Latham Island.
This location did not become an Indian reserve,
but is rated as "land reserved for Indian housing."

The Department of Indian Affairs
built ten five- by eight-metre plywood cabins,
and, to brighten this deportation camp,
painted the cabins in different colours.
Hence the name "Rainbow Valley,"
though most whites called it "Squaw Valley."

Yellowknife town had been all spruced up for the Queen,
some roads repaved and some buildings renovated.
Canadian and British flags flew everywhere.
City hall had not spent a cent in Rainbow Valley.
No garbage pick up, and no improvement on its mud trail
where, in some places, two cars couldn't pass each other.

"Why the heck does she want to go there?"

But the royal limousine drove there
and stopped at the lowest part of the valley.
The Queen and Prince Philip got out of the car
among children who put aside their homemade toys.

"Where are you coming from?"
"What's your name?"

More children gathered and shook hands,
followed by their parents
who had noticed something unusual.

I climbed down from my little house on top of the hill:

"Not one reporter is there,
and the Indians don't have cameras.
I am a good photographer.
What an opportunity!"

Fortunately, I decided not to intrude
on the only private hour
the Queen could enjoy in her four-day visit.
I was too far away to hear any of the conversation,
but at one point, the Queen turned to Alice:

"Are there any of your children here?"

"Yes, Freddy here, and Cecilia,
little Charlie there, and Jimmy,
Teddy behind, Archie over there,
and baby Jonas with me."

The Queen glanced right and left:

"That's quite a few.
How many children do you have?"

"Seventeen."

"Seventeen!"

"Yes, but there are three sets of twins."

"You must be a hard-working woman."

"And you, how many children do you have?"

"I have four children: Charles, Anne, Andrew
and Edward, the youngest, who is six."

"Four children? That's all!"

Moonlight

"Did you see the full moon last night?"

"No time, Jazzan.
In fact, I was at the library
studying about stars and planets.
Do you know that from the earth,
we can see fifty-nine per cent of the moon surface
which is composed of basic silicates."

"Ah?"

"The moon's diameter is 3,476 kilometres,
its mountains reach 8,000 metres,
and temperatures range from +125 to -175 degrees."

"Ah?"

"The moon travels on its orbit at one kilometre per second,
and the lunar phases repeat themselves
in an average of twenty-nine days, twelve hours
and forty-four minutes.

"Ah?"

"Did you know all those data?"

"I didn't know any."

"So, do you know anything at all about the moon?"

"Oh yes, it is so beautiful and mysterious!"

Mining

During the 1970 National Mining Week,
the manager of Giant Mine had invited the local Dene
to a public meeting at the Yellowknife Hotel.

"Some of you remember
when Giant Mine started in the mid-forties.
I feel sad that, after twenty-five years,
only two or three Dene work for us.
There is plenty of employment for you,
and you know what we do at Giant."

"Oh yes, you go way deep, you dig the rocks out,
and you pile them outside."

"But in those rocks, there is gold dust,
and we collect it."

"What do you do with that dust?"

"When we have enough,
we melt it into gold bricks."

"What do you do with those bricks?"

"We ship them to Ottawa."

"What do they do with those bricks in Ottawa?"

"In Ottawa,
the Bank of Canada has built deep basements
with thick concrete walls and heavy steel doors.
They pile up our gold bricks in those basements."

"Quite interesting!
but I don't see myself
digging gold out of the ground in Yellowknife,
to put it back into the ground in Ottawa!
You see, sir, I like to work for something useful."

Me?

"Gina, I'm so happy to see you again."

"Me, too, René,
 and I want to tell you a story."

"Please, go ahead, I love stories."

"Two months ago, I visited Northern Ontario,
 and I happened to meet Marg."

"Lucky you!"

"And we talked and talked,
 and, at one point, I asked her:

'Marg, do you know René?'

'Yes, I do.'

'How would you describe him?'

'René?
Oh, he likes to colour outside of the lines.'"

Manon

Manon,

care,
love,
gift,

pain,
trouble,
anxiety,

tease,
caress,
laughter,

charm,
wonder,
passion,

might,
vigour,
energy,

mind,
wisdom,
insight,

ice and fire,
rock and wind,
water and wine,

what I am not,
what I can be,

Manon,
for better or for worse,
for richer and poorer,
in sickness and in health,

Manon I never knew,
Manon I never married,

I love you.

Manobos

Wearing shorts, a T-shirt and a straw hat,
    I was riding the back of a motorcycle.
The temperature was thirty-two degrees Celsius,
    and, again and again, I tried to persuade myself
    that it was December 28.
My driver, Garry, was a Canadian Scarboro missionary
    in Opis, province of Bukidnon, Philippines.

At Namnam, we crossed a river without a bridge,
    and the previously rough trail narrowed into a path.
Eighteen kilometres from San Fernando
    we reached Opis, a village of forty huts,
    inhabited by tribal Manobos.

        'Tribal' people are aboriginal people,
            while 'Filipinos' means people of mixed blood,
            following the occupation of the Philippines
            first, by Spain, and, later on, by the U.S.A.

Garry, unwilling to influence the Manobos,
    had no watch, no radio, no camera, no tape recorder.
His hut was decorated with four cups,
    three plastic plates, three empty tin cans,
    one water pail, and two cooking pots.
Still, children reminded him:

        "You have beautiful things."

A few women went bare breasted and some wore jewelry.
One woman's arm, from wrist to elbow,
    was adorned by forty copper and two shell bracelets.
Older women wore thirty strings of beads
    tied at both ends to a wooden button
    inserted in their stretched earlobes.

I was told that young people married between the ages of fifteen and twenty.
Promiscuity and adultery were forbidden,
and punished by exile, or even death.

I showed photographs of Canadian Dene,
and everyone smiled at the similarity of features:

"Look at this boy, just like young Tabo here."

"This old lady looks like my grandmother."

Consequently, I was named:

"The one who lives with the Canadian Manobos."

A young, handsome man looked attentively
at the photograph of Bella, a pretty Dene girl.
He was one of the two Opis residents
who could speak a few words of English:

"I would like to marry this girl."

"She lives fifteen thousand kilometres from here."

His face dropped, but his mind kept working:

"How much would it cost to bring her here?"

I juggled air fares, exchange rates
and the price of local commodities:

"About the price of six carabaos."

The young man sadly shook his head:

"It's too much, too much."

***

Ten years later, I visited San Fernando again
    but I never reached that young man's village.
Garry had returned to Canada,
    and I inquired from Fr. Jim and Fr. Roger:

"I wonder if that young Manobo man got married."

"We don't know, there're no more Manobos in Opis."

"What happened?"

"Christian Filipinos from the Visaya islands
    came and took all the Manobo land.
Something like the settlers
    colonizing the Canadian prairies in the late 1800s."

"Opis seemed to be a healthy type of village."

"Yes, but the pagan Manobos had no land title.
Christians got titles to the land,
    and now, Opis is a Filipino village.
I feel sorry for the Manobos."

"I feel sorry for the Christians!"

Malo

Délı̨ne (Fort Franklin) was so delightful in May!
The snow had melted away, the air was crystalline,
and daylight lasted all 'night.'
Dene men and older boys had scattered far away
near rivers and small lakes
to harvest beaver and muskrat.

Sahtú (Great Bear Lake) rested yet under two metres of ice
but the open water along the shore widened daily.
Children jumped in and out of the icy water,
and stretched on the sandy shore to warm up.

Thirty metres separated the mission from the lake.
In that space, Malo had erected a small log building.
He had built most of his scant furniture,
and hammered a forty-five-gallon oil drum into a stove.

Malo was everybody's friend,
but he lived by himself.
His wife had died in 1935,
and their only daughter lived in Yellowknife.

Malo and I worked together frequently.
Every winter, we cut cords and cords of firewood
and hauled them with the mini-tractor
which replaced the mission dogs in the late sixties.
Malo had lived everywhere as a hunter, prospector, surveyor,
guide, trapper, miner, carpenter and fisherman.
And could he ever tell stories!

One night in May—
night only according to the clock—
I was sound asleep,
but in my sleep I heard faint noises
which stopped, and started again:
knock, knock, knock ... knock, knock, knock ...

"Am I awake, or asleep and dreaming?"

In those days, we never locked the doors,
  and I slept in the room nearest to the main door.
Whether awake or asleep I asked:

"Is there someone here?"

"Yes, it's me."

"Who is me?"

"It's me, Malo."

My watch indicated 2 a.m.

"Good morning, Malo, are you looking for something?"

Malo, in his softest voice:

"I'm sorry to disturb you.
I know you need to sleep like everyone else.
If you don't sleep at night,
  you cannot work during the day,
  but I thought that I should come and wake you up,
  because you may be able to help me."

"Something happened?"

"Yes, my house is on fire."

Those words jerked me awake,
  and propelled me out of bed into my trousers:

"Malo, grab this extinguisher here,
  and I'll take the one in the kitchen."

A hot fire in the stove had burned a hole in the floor.
The fire was spreading under the house,
  but we put it out in no time.

Lucky!

Lucky sand so soft!
Lucky rose so fragrant!
Lucky butterfly so graceful!

Lucky ant, you work tirelessly!
Lucky fish, you live under water!
Lucky eagle, you fly into the sun!
Lucky squirrel, you climb so playfully!

Lucky sun to be life giving!
Lucky water to adopt any shape!
Lucky clouds to hang on so lazily!
Lucky mountains to withstand the fiercest storms!

And suddenly I heard:

sand,
rose,
butterfly,
ant,
fish,
eagle,
squirrel,
sun,
water,
clouds,
mountains,
singing together:

"Lucky René to be you!"

Lice

In Kin-Iway, way up in the Filipino Cordillera,
  an adult education teacher shared his problem with me:

"When my students came, they had lice,
  but after three days, they had no lice,
  so I had to get some lice for them.
There are different kinds of lice,
  but we couldn't afford first class lice,
  so I told the merchant that ordinary lice would do.
In fact, the students were happy with the lice I bought.
I told them that I wouldn't buy any more lice,
  and that they'll have to manage with the lice they have."

Luckily, I remembered
  that the teacher was a Korean
  who pronounces 'r' as 'l'.

Living

When I arrived in Rádęlı̨ Kǫ́ (Fort Good Hope) in 1953,
I was ignorant of everything of the K'áshot'ı̨ne,
of their history, of their values,
of their 100,000 square kilometre territory.

Adele volunteered as my history and geography professor:

"Me and my husband,
we used to trap all winter long.
Sometimes way up the Mountain River,
close to the Yukon border.
At times, to the south, close to Nóhfee Kʔé Godé (Loche Lake).
Some winters, we lived near K'áhbamı̨́túé (Colville Lake)
nearly two hundred kilometres to the north-east.
Good fishing there, and usually lots of caribou,
good fur country, too, around Lac des Bois.
Or we travelled North four or five days by dog team,
to Tuk'á Túé (Loon Lake), Roʔe Tué (Rorey Lake),
and Fíchʔélejéé Tué (Canoe Lake).
We had good dog teams in those days,
and good legs and good snowshoes.
My husband, he was lucky at moose hunting,
probably because he was smart and not lazy.
Me, too, I was good at snaring rabbits,
shooting ptarmigan and partridge,
setting and visiting fishnets.

"When the trapping season was over,
we returned to the village for a while.
Right after Easter, we moved to Tuyahta,
you know, way up the Ts'udé Nı̨lı̨né (Ramparts River),
the country with thousands of small lakes.
Hard travelling because the snow was melting,
but daylight all night,
lots of ducks, geese, beaver and muskrat.
Ha! Spring time! The whole world and us, too,
we were frenzied with light and warmth.

"Right after the ice broke up,
we paddled back to the village.
Then, we camped up Dehcho (Mackenzie River),
below the big rapid,
and the whole summer, we dried fish for the winter.
In a good summer, we made eighty bales of dryfish,
you know, with one hundred and twenty fish in a bale.
It was something to clean and open up all those fish,
to hang them in the sun, and later in the smoking tent.
Came fall, off we were to the trapping grounds.
We were young and smart in those days,
and me and my husband, we raised five children."

I couldn't keep my feelings to myself:

"You and your husband,
you must have worked so hard all your life!"

Adele smiled, and shook her head,
possibly wondering if I would ever understand:

"No! I've told you, we never worked,
we lived in the bush all the time."

Le Benj

May 1940! It's useless to fight any more.
The German army has already invaded half of France.
A few days ago, tanks rolled past my home,
    and for the first time, I saw my father crying.
He had fought in the 1914-1918 war,
    supposed to be *'la der des ders,'*
    "la dernière des dernières guerres,"
    "the last of the last wars."

Today I am with my brothers in *Le Fuiteau*,
    a cluster of farm houses and barns,
    in the middle of a rich farming country.

A cloud of dust draws nearer over the dirt road.
Nobody says anything, but everyone knows:
The German armoured cars
    have reached even this small village
    way far from the main highways and towns.

The monsters, the noise and the dust
    stop in the middle of the village.
Some farmers go home and close their doors,
Others wander around as if nothing happened.

Benjamin, whom everyone calls *'Le Benj,'*
    stands in front of his house,
    and waves his arms:

        "Come on, boys, come in and have a drink."

Clementine, his wife, whispers to his ear:

        "Shut up, *Le Benj*, these are the Germans."

        "I know, I know. Come in, boys, and have a drink."

"*Le Benj,* they're our enemies."

"I know those people, we fought the last war together,
  la Grande Guerre, the Great war."

"Yes, *Le Benj,* but you were not on the same side."

"That's O.K. All soldiers should be friends.
Soldiers are not responsible for wars,
  they don't profit from wars,
  they only suffer and die."

Le Benj didn't live to see
  the Franco-German pact and the European community.
He was fifty years ahead of his time.

Joseph

It's been a year since Jesus left home.
The emptiness is closing all around me.
I miss my baby, my little boy,
  my apprentice, my partner, my friend.

He was still very small when he told me:

> "I am glad you called me Jesus. I like my name."

And a few months later:

> "Joseph, how come I wasn't born in Nazareth?"

I talked to him about our trip to Bethlehem.
I had never told anybody about that journey.
If people knew a little about our story,
  they'd probably stretch it wildly.

My little boy and I, hand in hand,
  we used to climb the hill behind Nazareth.
We honoured sunrise and sunset,
  we felt the breeze, we stood still for a long time.
One evening, Mary, a bit impatient:

> "Why were you so long? What were you doing?"

And Jesus, all smiles:

> "Daddy showed me how to be alive
>   as the clouds and the olive trees are alive."

For thirty years, Mary, Jesus and I,
  we helped each other to discover gifts
  we didn't even know lived in us.
What a happy and joyful family we created!

You should have heard the three of us laughing
the day Mary found a small coin she had lost.

We enjoyed visiting my father Jacob on his farm.
One spring day, my dad was sowing wheat in his field,
and Jesus rushed to me:

"Why is grandpa throwing away all those grains?"

I explained to him how seeds must die,
and become wheat, vegetables, or tall trees.
I knew that he understood me well.

My Jesus was seven years old
when we sailed together in Jotham's boat
across the Sea of Galilee.
A storm flared up, and Jesus held my arm with both hands:

"Joseph, are you scared?"

"A little bit. Yes. And you, Jesus, are you scared?"

"Me? No, you are with me."

I raised my boy well, and he raised me well also.
I know he felt secure at home,
and just as secure when he left us.
He listened to me carefully,
but I let him make his own decisions:

"If you mean 'yes,' say 'yes'; if it's 'no,' say 'no,'
and always say 'yes' to yourself."

I always helped the sick, the poor,
those who suffer and cry.
I knew that Jesus would follow my example.
He's been good at fixing everything bent or broken.
He's been good with people, too.

One morning, on our way to repair Hezron's roof,

Jesus walked towards a leper.

"Jesus," I said, "it's against our law."

"Why?"

Another day, Jesus witnessed his first funeral:

"Why do people die?"

and after the stone sealed the tomb:

"When will he come out?"

"Never," I said.

"Why not?"

I hear about Jesus once in a while,
but he has departed in many ways.
At the Cana wedding,
I knew that nothing would be the same again.
Jesus, he does see a new earth and a new world.
Old man Joram told me:

"Your Jesus, he's become a prophet,
and he may even stand as tall as Moses."

But some of our relatives laugh at him:

"What does he know? He's only a carpenter's son."

It hurts me. It's great to be a carpenter
or a carpenter's son.
I felt so proud when customers told me:

"You taught Jesus so well,
he works as well as you do."

My father died at fifty-four,
    and I am nearly that old myself.
Already, my muscles soften, my strength ebbs out,
    but living away from Jesus is my greatest pain.
Sometimes, Mary reminds me of Simeon's words:

"Sorrow will break your own heart."

It can't be. The Lord is a loving God
    who doesn't make people suffer.

Jesus, where are you tonight?

Iraq

1991: "Iraq is our enemy,
    and we, the Free World, must destroy it."

Iraq and the U.S.A. are super-armed,
    and both are reluctant to start a war,
    as even the winner could suffer a lot.
So, let Canada alone declare war on Iraq.

As Canada cannot invade Iraq,
    we'll invite Iraq to invade Canada.
As most Canadian submarines
    are in the West Edmonton Mall,
    Iraqi superships could land at the same time
    in Québec on the Saint Lawrence River,
    in Bathurst Inlet on the Arctic Ocean,
    and in super-natural Vancouver harbour.

Not speaking French, English, or Inuktitut,
    the Iraqis will be bored in no time.
They will call home for reinforcements,
    at least to have people to talk with.
Soon, thousands of Iraqi soldiers
    will look all over for the Canadian army
    which will be smart enough not to show up.

Some Iraqis will find their way to Ottawa,
    and witness Question Period.
Others will visit B.C.'s Fantasy Garden,
    and Bill Van der Zalm's fantasy legislature.
They'll discover that politics can be a lot of fun,
    and they will demand a similar government for Iraq.

The Defence Department's secret service
    will organize banquets and receptions for the Iraqis.
We will treat them to Arctic char, pea soup,
    Prairie beef, Ontario wine and Pacific salmon,
    until they grow so obese
    that they can't buckle their war belts.
When the Iraqis return home, they'll demand similar food,
    and the whole Iraqi army will have to be demobilized
    to produce all the needed food.

Some Iraqis won't even want to go back home,
    and they will invite their relatives to Canada.
And that's when we get them:
We'll give a cat to every Iraqi family.
Those people have suffered so many restrictions
    that they don't know anything about modern shopping.
They will spend all their time in supermarkets,
    unable to choose between forty-three kinds of cat food.
They won't have a minute to think of war!

At one point we'll have to come to our senses,
    and remember that war has been declared.
Neither Canadian nor Iraqi soldiers want to die.
Hopefully, they will agree that the war will be won
    by the country whose politicians tell the best lies.
We would have a 50/50 chance.

P.S. Unfortunately, that plan was rejected,
        and replaced by the Gulf War.
    Canada spent $1 billion.
    183,000 people were killed,
        half of them civilians.

Integration

"I am fed up with multiculturalism,
ancestral values and foreign cultures.
All people in Canada
should be Canadians, that's all."

"Dave, what do you mean?"

"People can do as they please in Europe or in Asia,
but, when they come to Canada,
they should behave like all Canadians."

"Do you mean that Poles, Arabs and Chinese
should forget their customs and languages?"

"Exactly, and also Hindus, Haitians and Italians.
When they arrive in our country,
they should give up their own culture and history,
and follow Canadian ways and values."

"You mean that all immigrants
should forget where they came from?"

"Exactly. They should integrate
into the Canadian ways which have been successful
for over one hundred years."

"Do you also mean that in 1492,
when Columbus' sailors landed in America,
they should have forgotten about Spain,
Spanish culture and Spanish language?
Are you saying that, five hundred years ago,
when the Spaniards landed in Indian country,
they should have adopted Indian values,
learned Indian languages and cultures,
and followed Indian laws and traditions
which had been tested for ten thousand years?"

"What nonsense!
How can you be so ridiculous?"

Interculture

Every July, from 1982 to 1992,
I invited fifteen Southern Canadians
to participate in a two-week Denendeh Seminar.
After three days in Yellowknife,
each group visited a small village for one week
to meet the Dene on their own land.

In 1982, our group flew from Yellowknife to Norman Wells
while five Dene drove five aluminum boats
upstream from Rádęlı̨ Kǫ́ (Fort Good Hope) to meet us.
At Norman Wells, four visitors boarded each boat,
possibly wondering about such small craft
for a two-hundred kilometre journey
down Dehcho (Mackenzie River)
which, in places, widens to five kilometres.

We drove by Ogilvie Island, and by Carcajou Ridge,
where Dehcho flows straight for twenty kilometres.
We reached the Sans Sault Rapid,
so named because it is much less dangerous
than the next rapids near Rádęlı̨ Kǫ́.
The cliff on the right rises one hundred metres,
in front of a five-hundred-metre limestone ridge.
We drove on the left side of the river,
as the high curly waves snarl only on the right side.

Further down, we all drove ashore,
made tea and cooked a few fish the Dene way,
seemingly totally unorganized but very efficient.

We tried to keep eye contact with the other boats
but suddenly the kicker on the last boat sputtered and quit.
'Kicker' is the northern name for outboard motors
that need to be cranked with a rope
and kick back when they don't feel like starting.

In the middle of the river, under a brilliant sun,
boat and passengers, enveloped by a sudden silence,
drifted with the seven-kilometre per hour current.
From the bottom of the boat, Ernest, the driver,
retrieved a screwdriver and a pair of pliers
and whatever he did, the kicker buzzed again.

Above Wolf Island, the same kicker quit again.
Three visitors, unaware of the distance left,
and possibly afraid to say the wrong thing,
kept an apprehensive silence,
but Sylvia turned towards the pilot-mechanic:

"Excuse me, sir, what will we do
if the motor doesn't start?"

"Well, we'll paddle to shore and we'll make tea."

Nobody could voice their feelings any further
because the kicker started again,
and ran smoothly all the way to Rádęlį Kǫ́.

We camped in two former portable classrooms
and lived one week of informal interculturation.
Many Dene joined us for meals,
for serious discussions,
for walks through the village,
and for picnics at the Xayįts'á Nilįné (Hare River).

Suddenly the last evening was upon us,
the last meal together and the last stories.
Jane had already gathered her children, ready to go home,
but she stopped to shake hands with Dermot:

"Will all you people come again next summer?"

"I doubt it. We are not rich people,
we came from all across Canada,
and I doubt we can afford to come again."

"That's too bad. We were happy to see you."

"We, too, we appreciated the Dene hospitality."

"So, you won't come again, will you?"

"It seems you would like us to come again.
Why?"

"You see, you're the first white people
who come to our village
without trying to tell us what we should do."

Insomnia

I had always been told that
older people don't sleep as long as younger ones,
or that they wake up more often during the night.
Now, I know it is true.

I didn't run a Gallup poll,
but I asked a few friends, those my age,
what they do when they wake up during the night.

Erma: "It's awful, I turn and toss."

Nancy: "I listen to good music on the radio."

Jimmy: "I have a cup of milk, maybe with a cookie."

Agnes: "I watch a funny VHS movie."

Betty: "I say my rosary, maybe two."

Bernie: "I read a book, a kind of light book."

Pascal: "I keep breathing in and breathing out."

Honesty

People from various countries
and from different backgrounds
made Aklavik a friendly town in the 1950s.
Most residents were characters,
but Jim was *the* character.

Jim had just climbed the river bank,
pushing a wheelbarrow full of white fish.
People stopped him on the road:

"Jim, can you sell me a fish?"

"Yes, a dollar a fish."

More buyers, same question, same answer,
until Tiny Scott asked:

"Jim, can you sell me a fish?"

"Yes, fifty cents."

Tiny left with his fish,
and people grumbled:

"Jim, you charge us a dollar a fish,
and only fifty cents to Tiny."

"Wait a minute! I'll explain it to you.
You see, I had not one fish in my own net,
so I got all those fish from Tiny's net.
I couldn't charge him the same price.
One has to be honest!"

Holiday

"Good morning, Cliff, where have you been?
I haven't seen you for a while."

"Oh, Lloyd, I was so tired,
I was afraid my heart would give up on me.
I took two months off, went to a quiet place,
visited friends and did nothing."

"That's too bad."

"I couldn't take it any more.
I had to go and rest."

"But if you had stayed here,
you may have had a real heart attack.
Imagine that for business!
Ambulances, taxis and cars for your friends,
probably medevac jet plane to Edmonton,
hospital for days ... or even weeks,
fancy equipment buzzing all over,
doctors, nurses, all kinds of specialists,
surgeons, radiologists, cardiologists.
Phone calls all over the country,
mail and presents from your friends,
flowers and get well cards ... Wow!
How much did you spend on your holiday?"

"All together with the trip?
About $1,500."

"A good heart attack would have been worth
one hundred times more than that to our economy!
If all people were to care for their health the way you do,
how could we expect our economy to recover?"

Hockey

When I moved to Yellowknife in 1970,
I settled in T'èʔehda (Dettah),
a small Dene community
without phone and electricity,
and without a permanent road to Yellowknife,
about twenty-five kilometres away.

I was fascinated by the games
Dene children invented according to the seasons.
It was perfectly safe for them
to play on the 'road' between the houses.
Joe owned the only truck in the village,
and snowmobiles had not arrived yet.

In winter, any stretch of road turned into an arena.
Children handmade their hockey sticks.
Blocks of firewood became goal posts.
Players wore moccasins and parkas,
and I couldn't figure out who was on what team,
and which official rules applied or did not apply.

One November afternoon, I decided to watch attentively.
The Eagles and the Ravens started with five players each.
The score climbed to 1-1.
Then, the Ravens scored twice in a row,
so they gave a player to the Eagles to even the chances.
Later on, the Eagles led by two goals,
and in turn, they gave one player to the Ravens.
Then I understood why the scores
were always so close: 2-1, 4-3, 5-4, 3-2,
and no team was ever really beaten.

Help

Conrad shouted with joy
for the salmon jumping up the waterfall.
He grieved at those washed down the river:

"What a pity!
Nobody helps those fish. I will."

He caught a salmon in his old angler's net,
and carried it three hundred metres over the portage.
He gently let the fish into the water
and watched it go, but it was already dead:

"Stupid fish!"

The next day, he bought a new nylon net
with a chrome frame and a colourful plastic handle.
He carried a fish to the top of the waterfall ...
The fish died.

Conrad knew he needed help,
and the next day he brought five friends.
They each carried a fish upstream.
The six fish died.

Conrad concluded that the path was too narrow,
and they widened it into a road.
Carrying fish was so much easier now,
but the fish died just the same.

Conrad resolved:

"Not enough people know about us."

Soon, dozens of newspapers ran his story
under a bold headline: "People Helping Salmon."
Thousands read that article,
even Alebon, an old Dene, who commented to me:

"This is not a fish story, my friend.
This is history past and present."

Guitar

In the 1950s, Rádęlı̨ Kǫ́ (Fort Good Hope) was quiet in winter time,
without cars, trucks, or even snowmobiles:
the first skidoos were born in 1961.
Hundreds of narrow paths crisscrossed the village,
wide enough for dog-teams and toboggans,
and for people to walk 'Indian file.'
In October, after all the lakes were frozen,
most Dene families left the village for their trapping grounds.

Once a week, the Community Club showed a movie at the school.
Each September, the last boat of the season
brought fifty 16-mm films to be shown through the year.
Those films were probably not needed in Southern Canada
as we shipped them back by boat the following June.
One winter, we saw the forty-three episodes of *Zorro,*
or was it fifty-one or thirty-nine?

Once in a while, traditional drums,
or the two guitars and the fiddle of 'Ed and the Hopers,'
filled with joy the old log building named Community Hall.

Bingos were still unknown in Denendeh,
probably because most Dene never handled cash,
but used only credit and debit vouchers at both stores.

One store, Kakfwi's 'independent' trading post
depended less on the number of furs purchased
and on the amount of goods sold,
than on the level of local unpaid debts
and on the bookkeeping style of an Edmonton wholesaler.

The other store, the Hudson's Bay,
significantly crowned the top of a small hill
in the centre of the village.

On Sunday afternoon, or in the evening moonlight,
young and not-so-young people gathered near the Bay
with small sleighs or large toboggans.

A steep path ran eastwards
towards Paul's house near the bottom of the hill.
The challenge for overloaded toboggans
was to manage a turn to the right before hitting Paul's house,
and to slide down the bank of the small creek
all the way to the deep snow on top of the ice.
Toboggans often overturned before reaching their goal,
scattered their passengers into the snowbanks,
and allowed teenagers to get closer to each other.

One afternoon, a young boy sat on a guitar,
held the stem with both hands, and zipped down the slope.
I noticed his mother, Judy, standing near me:

"Is that your little Jimmy?"

"Yes."

"He's sliding down on a guitar."

"Yes."

"Whose guitar is it?"

"His big brother's."

"He may break the guitar."

"Yes, could be."

That evening, I lay in bed
after the village had disappeared in silence.
I visualized little Jimmy,
his father, mother, brothers and sisters,
lying in their sleeping bags next to each other.
I could nearly hear Judy
telling one of her delightful stories:

“Long, long time ago, a little boy
    lived near a lake far away from here.
That little boy, long ago and far away.
    I guess he didn’t know
    some things are very solid,
    and others break easily.
Anyway, that little boy far away ...”

Of course,
    Judy never linked the old story to Jimmy.
Oh no!

Gold

Joe was the best hunter, the best fisherman,
 the best river pilot, and the best storyteller.
One day, he arrived in a solemn mood.

"You know Noël in Tulíta (Fort Norman)
He's never been a go-getter,
 but usually, he's lucky.
Last May, we had tea together:

"'Joe, I want to show you something.'

"He got his hunting packsack from his warehouse:

"'Joe, a few weeks ago,
 I was hunting in Blackwater country.
I found something that I've never seen before.
It looks like a kind of metal
 that melted and hardened again.
It is spread flat on the ground.
 Quite large too, about twenty steps long
 and as wide as two axe handles.
Nothing grows on it, but it's not stone.
With my axe, I cut a small chunk of that stuff,
 and I want you to look at it.'

"The lump was as big as a small egg.
It was some kind of metal, but rather soft;
 I could see the scratches of the axe blade.

"'Noël,' I said, 'I want to send a small bit
to the Assay Office in Yellowknife.'

"Two weeks later, the report came back:

"'Guess what, Noël, the stuff is pure gold.'

"'Well, Joe, here is where I got it,
right on the south shore of Taloka Lake,
left side of the small river mouth.
Go and get it if you feel like it,
and if you make some money from it,
I trust you'll give me some.'

"René, I don't know how deep is the gold,
maybe six, seven inches, maybe one foot,
even if it's only two inches, it's worth it.
Noël said it's a solid mass, right on the ground.
I know that a small float plane
can land on this lake.
Right now, I don't have any money,
but we could go partners.
You charter the plane and we'll share.
You also buy one of those new chain saws.
We'll saw the gold into square foot chunks,
and we can load them in the plane."

Chain saws were still unknown in Délı̨ne.
Without providing any unnecessary information,
I wrote the bishop's bursar that I needed a chain saw.
It arrived two weeks later,
a twenty-pound yellow McCulloch.
We were ready for serious planning!
A Norman Wells airline quoted us a price
for a round trip to such a distance.
We set a date, and we had completed our preparations
when a gale started to blow and lasted for one week.
This is not unusual on Sahtú (Great Bear Lake),
and we waited without any worry;
the gold was not going to melt.

The weather had just started to improve
when Joe showed up at the mission:

"I am in a bad fix. I need some advice."

Joe handed me a telegram
from the NTCL, the Northern Transportation Company Ltd:

A U.S. oil company gave us the contract
to take three barges of drilling equipment
down Dehcho to Tuktoyaktuk.
Thence, five hundred miles westwards
along the Arctic coast to Alaska,
and about one hundred miles
up the Colville River.
Nobody has ever piloted a boat up that river,
and there is no chart, no navigation markers.
Joe, you're the only person
who can pilot those barges up that river.
We know you're kind of retired
but can you show up in three days?

"It bothers me because we planned that gold trip,
but NTCL has always been good to me.
They gave me employment for many years.
Mind you, I did a lot for them, too.
I can't let them down. I'll go up the Colville River.
We'll go for the gold when I come back.
I'm sure Noël won't tell anybody."

Joe piloted the boat and barges up the Colville River:

"Nasty muddy water," he later reported to me,
"a lot of eddies and massive landslides,
but I never touched a rock or a sandbar."

By then, it was fall, a lot of rain, a bit of snow:

"Not pleasant weather to work outside.
Next spring we'll go for that gold."

The chain saw came in handy to cut our firewood.

Winter and spring rolled over,
and many more winters and springs.
It was only last January that I remembered
about that gold find thirty-five years ago.

Now, Joe lives in an old folks' home,
I have retired in Łútsel K'e (Snowdrift),
both of us too old to be concerned about gold.

Genesis

In September 1975,
five Canadian Christian Churches
established an ecumenical coalition Project North
to work in solidarity with aboriginal nations,
and to promote their creative activities.
It also called southern Christians to “a conversion
within our social and economic structures
whereby policy making and decision making
will begin to reflect and make practical
the values of justice, dignity
and fulfilment of every human being.”

I never held any title within that coalition,
but, for years, I was fortunate
to be involved in many of its projects
and to be challenged by its new vision —
I mean, its two-thousand-year-old vision.

For eight years, Clifton Monk represented
the Lutheran Church in America Canada Section,
on Project North’s board of directors.
He chaired the coalition
from April 1981 to September 1983.

During Clif’s retirement party,
this staunch Lutheran and competent organizer
took the opportunity to introduce a note of humour
by reading the first chapter of the Bible:

> In the beginning, the heavens and the earth were without form, so God created a small committee. God carefully balanced the committee according to race, sex, ethnic origin and economic status in order to interface pluralism with the holistic concept of self-determination according to the adjudicatory guidelines. Even God was impressed and so ended the first day.

Then God said: "Let the committee draw up a Mission Statement." And behold, the committee decided to prioritize and strategize. God called this process empowerment and thought it sounded pretty good, and so ended the second day.

Then God said: "Let the committee determine goals and objectives, and engage in long-range planning." Unfortunately, a debate as to the semantic differences between goals and objectives pre-empted almost all of the third day. Although the question was never satisfactorily resolved, God thought the process was constructive, and so ended the third day.

Then God said: "Let there be a workshop in which the committee can envision functional organization and engage in consistent planning." The committee considered adjustment of priorities and the consequential alternatives to program directions. God saw that this was good, and that it was even worth all the coffee and the donuts he had to supply. So ended the fourth day.

And God said: "Let the committee's desires be implemented consistent with the long-range planning and strategy." The committee considered guidelines, linkages, structural sensitivities, alternative and implementational models. God saw that this was very democratic, and so ended the fifth day.

On the sixth day, the committee agreed on criteria for the adjudicatory assessment and evaluation. This wasn't the agenda that God had planned, and he wasn't able to attend all the sessions because he used the afternoon to create sun and moon, day and night, stars, seasons, seas, trees, birds, reptiles, fish, animals and human beings.

On the seventh day, God rested, and the committee submitted its recommendations. It turned out that the recommended form for most creatures was nearly identical to the way that God had already made them. So the committee passed a resolution commending God for his implementation according to the guidelines.

And God caused a deep sleep to fall upon the committee members.

Free Flour

My friend Angus is not an elder yet,
but he started another old story:

"In those days, us children,
    we always helped the old people.
We got water from the lake for them.
We collected firewood along the shore,
    we cut it and carried it to their homes.
Sometimes they gave us a piece of bannock,
    or a bit of dry fish or dry meat,
    but, even if they gave us nothing,
    we still helped them.

"One day, when I was about twelve years old,
    I cut firewood for Old Michel.
He gave me some bannock, and he warned me:

"'It's OK to eat that bannock,
    because I bought the flour myself,
    but never accept bannock from Treaty Indians.
The Indian Agent gives them flour for free
    though he gives nothing to us Métis.
But the government puts something into that flour
    that makes people's minds get weak.

"'You know Gabe.
He has always been good to everybody,
    so the people elected him as Indian Chief.
The government started to give him free flour.
    he's still a good man, but he became a weak chief.'

"I always remembered Old Michel's words.
Even when I was really, really hungry,
    I never accepted bannock from Treaty Indians,
    and my mind is still strong to this day."

Frances

Theresa: "I'm so frustrated with Frances."

Charlie: "Last week, Frances came to my place,
and she just wanted to talk.
Finally, I had to send her home."

Jacquie: "Thursday, Frances showed up. I asked her:
'What do you want?'
'Nothing.'
'Good, because I have to go,
or I'll be late for bingo.'"

Larry: "Frances? What a big babbler."

Eileen: "Last night, Jenny called me to come
and see a video.
Frances was sitting silently,
so I left her alone at home
to see if she would ever make up her mind."

Alfred: "Every day in the past week,
I wasted an hour listening to Frances."

Louisa: "Sunday afternoon, Frances stood by the shore
and she asked me all kinds of questions,
but my family was waiting for me to go fishing."

On July 17, Frances killed herself.

Five women spent the afternoon
cleaning her body, ironing clothes and dressing her.
Two men spent hours making her coffin.

Twelve people spent half a day preparing food
for Frances' family and for visiting friends.
Fifty people stayed up most of the night for her wake.

Frances' auntie took four days off work
    and flew in from the city to attend the funeral.
Frances' sister, her husband and their children
    came from Vancouver for the funeral,
    and they remained five days.

It took four men five hours to dig Frances' grave.
The school, the offices, the village services
    closed down for half a day.
One hundred and fifty people
    attended the two-hour church service for Frances,
    and they prayed two more hours at the graveyard:

        "We all loved her so much."

Freedom Fighter

Leon had been drinking, but he walked straight:

"Father René, can you drive me to the Bailey's?"

Gordon Bailey was a Pentecostal minister
  and his wife Ruth was as dedicated as he was.
They moved from Manitoba to Denınu (Fort Resolution) in 1958
  and to Latham Island, Yellowknife, in 1963.
They lived mostly on faith.
They opened their house and their hearts
  to anyone in need of food or shelter.
Their house was overcrowded day and night
  but never too small for one more.

We started driving down Franklin Avenue:

"You know, Father, I'm not very smart,
I never went very much to school at all,
  but I was a good bush man.
Now, I'm hopelessly out of date,
  my own path is gone, nothing to follow.
I'm even useless to help in any Dene organization.
I know I drink a lot,
  and the whites, they shove me off the sidewalks,
  they laugh at me and they curse me.

"Yes, I'm killing myself slowly,
  but there's a war going on, and wars kill people.
The whites are destroying our nation.
They're too many, they're too smart for me.
Being drunk, acting stupid, and dying
  may be the only way
  I can help them look at themselves."

Leon died at the age of 50,
four months after our conversation.

Foreigners

After flying for thirteen hours from San Francisco
    and two more hours from Hong Kong,
    we entered the main hall of the Manila airport
    which is a dark massive concrete structure.

Soon we were surrounded by thousands of Filipinos
    of rather short stature and dark complexion.
It seemed that twenty family members attended
    any relative taking off or landing.

A woman arriving on the same flight stood by me,
    taller than I, with blue eyes and golden hair.
She half covered her face with her hands:

> "Oh my God,
> there are lots of foreigners in this country!"

Dollars

December snow and north wind
didn't prevent five children from roaming the streets.
They were all young, but old friends.

"Look on the sidewalk!" said Serge.

Clem was already running,
and picking up the twenty-dollar bill:

"Finders keepers."

"You're so greedy!"

All joined the clamour:

"We're together, so we should share."

"You talk of sharing only when you have nothing."

"Let's buy something."

"Money always burns your fingers."

"Let's get ice cream."

"Silly! It's thirty-five below."

"We'll take four dollars each."

"No, let's have fun together."

"Go to the movies?"

"We can slip in for free anyway."

"We'll discuss it tomorrow."

“Who will keep the money tonight?”

“I wouldn’t trust you.”

“Nor you.”

“Let’s open a bank account.”

“What’s the use to have money in a bank?”

“Let’s buy candies and chocolates.”

“You’re all stomach and no brain.”

“Well, let’s do something, anything.”

“What’s wrong with you? No time to think?”

“I know, let’s buy some 649 tickets.”

“What for?”

“We may win two hundred dollars,
    or even two thousand.”

“Shucks!
We just about destroyed our friendship
    for a lousy twenty.
What would happen to us
    if we had two thousand?”

Destiny

"Do you know any congregation
which sends missionaries to cold countries?"

"Yes," I was answered, "the Oblates."

I didn't want to serve as a priest in France,
nor to roast under the tropics,
so I joined the Oblates.

In February 1953, twelve of us, young Oblates,
had completed our studies
at the Solignac scholasticate.
Our Superior General in Rome
was to send us our 'obedience,' our first posting.
Father Brohan, our local Superior,
joyfully prepared for the solemnity:

"Many relatives and friends will come.
We need an outstanding personality to preside."

Cameroon was then a new Oblate mission,
the dream of the toughest missionaries.
Bishop Plumey, its leader, was visiting France
and he accepted Brohan's invitation eagerly.
His presence would advertise his mission,
and possibly secure some financial support.

But a few days before the great event,
Father Brohan was near despair:

"Bishop Plumey is sick and he cannot come.
Who could ever come on such a short notice?
Hum ... maybe Bishop Fallaize?"

Bishop Fallaize, almost blind and retired in Lisieux,
arrived two days before the great celebration
and chatted cheerfully with our superior:

"Father Brohan, I would like to know
where all these young boys are going.
I promise not to tell them,
but could you show me their obediences?"

Bishop Fallaize checked the twelve papers:
Cameroon, France, Cameroon, Laos,
Laos, France, Cameroon, France, Cameroon,
France, Cameroon, Basutoland:

"Well, Father Brohan, here are your papers.
I'm going back home."

"Bishop, what happened?"

"I spent thirty years in Northern Canada,
and not one of these boys is going there.
I'm not interested in your celebration."

"Please, Bishop, don't get hasty,
let's have a good sleep tonight,
and everything may look better tomorrow."

Fax machines and E-mail were not yet born,
but Fr. Brohan phoned our Rome headquarters:

"Anything you can do to please the old bishop?"

Our Superior General sympathized:

"Fumoleau has his obedience for Cameroon.
Erase that and replace it with Mackenzie.
Have a good day—Bishop Fallaize and all."

Cuddling

"Dear God,
I'm setting aside the next three hours
to prove my love for you.

"I will recount Genesis, Chapter 1,
to celebrate you as the Creator.

"I will recite the Song of Moses,
in Deuteronomy, Chapter 32.
You must love it so much!

"I will attend the half-hour church service.

"I will recite my rosary to celebrate Mary
who did such great things for you.

"I will sing the hymn 'How Great Thou Art.'
It is such beautiful praise for you!

"I will relate to you the story of the Last Supper,
from St. John's gospel, Chapters 13 to 17.

"Dear God, I really want to please you."

"If you want to do all that,
just go ahead, but ..."

"But what?"

"But would you mind if,
for the next three hours,
you and I, we just quietly cuddle up?"

Creation

I have been God from all eternity.
        It has to be from all eternity, there is nothing else,
        and I am still the only one who knows about it.
For a change, I would like to share my power and my goodness,
    to try something different, maybe create a world.

How does one create? It has never been done before!
        Is my imagination running wild?
        There is a problem with being all-powerful:
        One has too many choices and alternatives.

What to create? A world? What is a world?
There is not even a word for it.
I could start with creating stars, but what are stars?
Stars must be different from everything else,
    but there is nothing else yet.
How can stars be different from what does not exist?

How many stars will I need? A dozen or a few million?
What do numbers mean? I've never needed numbers before,
    and math has not yet been invented.
The problem with adding and multiplying
    is that one never knows when to stop.
        I will never be good with figures,
        They are too restrictive, they spoil infinity.

So, I will make a universe like eternity,
    with no boundary, no limit and no end.
        No, that will not work either: creatures cannot be eternal.

I want the greatest variety of creatures.
I will create millions of different things and animals ...
Here I am, stuck with figures again.
And what are things and animals?
Even I, I have never seen one thing or one animal.
I have never heard of feet, wings, fins and feathers.
Should animals crawl, fly, swim, or walk?
What colours match? I don't know colour yet.
What creatures should be solid or liquid,
cold or warm, small or big, inert or growing?
Why did I ever start imagining a creation?

I want every creature to be different and unique,
but all equal, not inferior or superior to others.
They must know they are all important to me,
because each one will be exactly as I make it to be.

Some creatures won't have much to say about their future,
and they will praise me in their own way.
Some will be more like me, with a lot of freedom,
knowing what helps them grow, what stifles them,
and learning to live with their choices.
I will tell them:
"You have to care for each other,
you've got the whole world in your hands."
They will also know that it is in my nature
to give them one chance after another.

I have been thinking ... All creatures will die.
Will I have to create new things over and over again?
That would take all my time!
Listen to me! I'm talking about past, present and future,
as if time existed at all.
This whole idea of creation is confusing me.
How could my creatures give life to others of their kind?
I don't know yet about seeds, eggs, male and female features.
I am getting into one problem after another.

I should forget about all the details.
I think the most glorious way for me to create
    is to make something small, really small,
    but full of love, and full of life,
    and to let it grow, evolve and develop on its own.
        I still have a problem: nothing can be small,
        because there is nothing big to compare it with.

I will trust and care for every one of my creatures,
    and their world will end up a success.
        Do not ask me how, but I will find my way.
        After all, I would not create anything that would fail.

Yes, creation is going to be quite a success!

Crack

Story first told at the Vancouver
Storytelling Festival, March 30, 1996

If you start from Vancouver and walk due north,
after three months, or four months if you walk slowly,
you will reach the village of Déline (Fort Franklin),
at the southwest corner of Sahtú (Great Bear Lake).

For the Dene who have lived there ten thousand years
Déline means "near the water that never freezes."
The name refers to the start of the Sahtú Dıé (Bear River)
which drains Sahtu water into Dehcho (Mackenzie River).

I lived in Déline from 1960 to 1968.
And there, my friends,
lake trout and white fish are so large and so plentiful
that we don't have to make up fish stories.
Thirty-, forty-, fifty-pounders are common.

On March 31, 1961,
that is thirty-five years ago tomorrow,
Leracko's wife checked her family's provisions:

"Not much meat left, not much fish either."

Leracko got the message:

"I'll go and set a fish hook."

A problem with setting fish hooks in March
is that the lake is covered with six feet of ice,
yes, my friends, over two metres of ice.
Leracko picked up his ice chisel,
and walked over the ice to a 'good spot,' one mile away.
An ice chisel is a sharp piece of three-inch wide steel
tied up to an eight-foot long handle.

We had no power tools in those days,
and to set a hook under the ice
we chiselled out a sixty-centimetre wide hole

Leracko was used to such a tedious job.
After a little more than two hours,
his ice chisel broke through the last centimetre of ice,
and the water rushed up to the top of the hole.
Leracko had wrapped a small fish over a four-inch hook.
and he tied the hook to a long, long line.
The trout is a bottom-feeder,
so Leracko tied a small stone to the line
to ensure the hook would sink
to about one foot above the bottom of the lake.

The next day, on the morning of April 1, 1961,
(everyone in Délı̨ne still remembers that date)
the east wind had turned into a gale,
but, at daybreak, Leracko walked to his hook.
He cleared the thin ice
which had built up over his hole
and he started to pull his line up:

"There's one for sure, must be a big one, too."

The fish pulled down, Leracko pulled up.
Down and up, down and up went the line,
until Leracko peered down the hole:

"Wow! a trout head wider than my hole."

Leracko allowed the trout to swim deeper,
and, proud but worried,
he tied the line to a small stick frozen in the ice.

"What if the trout gets away?
What if I cannot pull it out?"

The ice chisel danced and widened the hole,
struck the ice, chopped the ice,
struck and chopped, irresistible:

Crack!

The ice cracked open on both sides of the hole
two miles to the south shore,
two miles to the north shore.

"What's that? What did I do?
The crack is widening."

The fierce east gale
heaved and pushed this immense ice field,
split and shoved enormous ice cakes
towards the west shore of the bay.
Leracko breathed easier when he realized
that he stood on the solid side of the widening gap.

The other Dene, bewildered, lined up on the shore:

"The ice has never moved before the end of June.
What blessing or what disaster is visiting us?"

Leracko's wife shrilled through the gale rumble:

"My husband is on the ice visiting his hook."

I saw everybody, young and old, rushing by my window
and I put on my mukluks and my parka.
We all ran along the shore and then on the solid ice.

Leracko had managed to hang on to the line and to the trout.
When I got there, a dozen people
had just pulled the monstrous trout out of the water,
and loaded it onto a toboggan.
Then, they all shook their heads:

"How could such a line hold such a fish?"

Men and women, slow elders and frolicking children
processed back to the village.

We held a feast and a drum dance,
to celebrate the gigantic trout
and to thank Newhetsini
who had granted fish power and ice power to Leracko.

Did we ever rejoice over the ice-free bay:

"Now, we can use canoes to set fishnets and hooks.
No more holes to chisel through the ice!"

And, I'm telling you the truth,
the bay never froze again until the following winter.

Counselling

"Danny's dumped me. I hate him.
I hate school, I hate myself.
Fifteen is the worst age one can be.
Claire, do you feel like that sometimes?"

"I'm fifteen."

"What do you do when you're heartsick?"

"I talk to my counsellor."

"You have a counsellor?"

"In fact, I have two."

"You can go to one or to the other?"

"It depends."

"How often do you see them?"

"Whenever I feel like it."

"Don't you have to make appointments?"

"No. It's when I want to."

"Do they have a lot of experience?"

"Oh yes, years and years."

"But do they really know you?"

"Yes, for a long time."

"How much do they charge you?"

"Nothing."

"Gosh, I want to meet your counsellors.
What are their names?"

"Mom and Dad."

Co-op

In January 1961, Aklavik Constructors Company
was building a new airstrip in Norman Wells,
and the Délįne (Fort Franklin) Dene heard that
the company wanted to buy fish.
They borrowed fifty dollars, bought some trout,
shipped it, and sold it at fifty cents a pound.
By mid-February they had repaid their debt,
and already the books showed a profit of $89.
The airstrip was completed; the fish market disappeared.

In September 1961, the Dene tried handicraft marketing
and, in three months, bought and sold $132 of handicrafts.

Once a month, the Inuvik Indian agent visited Délįne,
and frowned at the new venture and at its success:

"Yes, Eskimos have started co-operatives,
but Indians are not able to do that."

Sixteen-year-old Johnny Tutcho
was the first secretary of the not-yet-born co-op.
Then, a local school student, Sarah Cleary,
took over for two years.

On June 14, 1963,
thirty-six members voted to organize
Great Bear Co-operative Association.
A month later, it was officially registered,
the first Indian co-operative in the N.W.T.
By then, Délįne people had earned $7,900 through their co-op.

From June to December 1963,
the co-op bought and sold $3,900 of handicrafts.
Due to shortage of cash, the co-op printed its own money:
coupons of five dollars, one dollar, and fifty cents.
The co-op bought handicrafts half in Canadian dollars,
and half in co-op money, valid at the co-op store.

In summer 1964, the co-op invested $3,000 in groceries
to be retailed in its own store.
Through 1964 the co-op sold $6,700 of general merchandise
and $7,700 of handicrafts,
and, at the end of the year, it could afford
to pay $1,000 dividends to its members.

In summer 1965, encouraged by its success,
the co-op ordered $8,000 worth of groceries.
Through 1965, the co-op sold $13,600 worth of handicrafts.
At the end of the year, it had assets worth $21,100.

The Great Bear Co-operative
has grown through fog, gales and sunshine.
In 1996, it returned, as dividends, $120,000 cash to its members.

***

I was privileged to live in Délįne in the 1960's,
and to witness the financial success of the co-op,
as well as its educational achievements.

I remember that the Great Bear Co-operative
hired a full time manager in fall 1967.
In spring 1968, some members were dissatisfied with him,
and, at a general meeting, they voted him out.
The following morning, two Dene arrived at the mission:

"The co-op manager, is he going to go?"

"Yesterday you voted to send him out."

"But you trained him, you worked with him.
Since he came, you and he were friends."

"Yes, we are friends,
and I think it's a mistake to make him leave."

"Are you going to make him stay?"

"As co-op members you are the only people
who can decide anything about your co-op."

"Is the government going to make him stay?"

"Nobody in the government
can go against what you decide."

"But the government can do whatever it wants."

"Not about your co-op.
Whatever you say, it's the law."

That same day, ten people asked me the same questions.

That was the first time the Dene experienced
that collectively they could have power over their own lives.

Jewels

Glenn and June entered the jewelry store.
They wore clean clothes, they held their heads straight,
  but obviously they had never been in such a sparkling world.
Their eyes had slowly gotten used to the luxury,
  when an elegant clerk approached them:

"Are you looking for something special?"

"Yes, a present for my wife," Glenn answered.

The clerk showed them to a display case.
Glenn looked at some price tags:

"Is that in dollars?"

"Yes, sir," answered the clerk.

One ring cost more than his monthly salary,
  and one bracelet more than his yearly income.
To their innocent questions the clerk politely answered:

"No, sir," or "Yes, madam."

June looked at her husband, wondering:

"People who buy those jewels,
  do they really love each other
  a thousand times more than we do?"

Finally, Glenn looked at the clerk:

"I don't know why we came here,
maybe only to dream for a while.
When we came in you must have known
we couldn't afford any of this,
but you were polite and showed us respect.
That's a real present in itself,
and we thank you."

Back on the busy sidewalk,
with people pushing right and left,
Glenn and June hugged passionately:

"Happy birthday, June, I love you.
You know, dear, even if we had the money,
nothing in there was good enough for you."

Civilization

"It's true. All of us, all the Dene,
we want to join your Western civilization."

"We trust that you are sincere,
but we doubt that you can be partners with us."

"Why not?"

"You see, your Dene languages don't have words
for all the things so essential to our civilization,
words like:

MX missiles,
strategic nuclear arsenal,
fragmentation weapons,
tactical nuclear warheads,
massive nuclear retaliation,
medium range missiles targeted by satellite,
strategy of suffocation,
nuclear holocaust,
horizontal nuclear proliferation,
detection-against-bombers systems,
nuclear escalation,
intercontinental ballistic missiles,
saturation bombing,
hyper-velocity pellets,
multiple independently targeted re-entry vehicles,
binary chemical weapons,
laser beam anti-ballistic weapons,
nuclear and tomahawk land attack missiles ...

"We feel sorry for all of you Dene folks.
But before you can be partners with us,
you'll have to modernize your languages,
and become civilized like us."

Charlie

My friend stopped me on the sidewalk:

"Father, can you help me?"

"Could be, Charlie, what for?"

"I want to pay my electricity bill."

"That's a good idea."

"But can you help me?"

"Well, what do you mean?"

"I've got empty beer bottles at my place.
You come with your little truck.
We'll take the bottles to the depot.
I'll sell them and I can pay my power bill."

"That's good thinking, Charlie.
I'll go to your place tomorrow about noon."

"Thank you, my friend."

Charlie walked away two steps, and turned back:

"Do you know what?
A few years ago, electricity was cheap.
I sold just a few empty beer bottles,
and that was enough to pay my bill.
Now, those bills have gone so high,
boy, I've got to drink a lot of beer."

Challenges

My good Spirit,

Teach me all the amazing truths
which I learned already.
Feed me all the exotic foods
I tasted so far.
Give me all the joys
I learned to cherish.

Lead me wherever you want
on the roads I travelled.
Take me to the highest point
which I chose myself.
Lead me on the wildest adventures
according to my careful plans.

Make me grow up
to the size I am.
Stretch me to the breaking point,
within the limits I set.
Test me with the challenges
I mastered already.

Heal me of all my addictions,
I mean, those I don't like.
Fill my cup to the brim
until I say "Enough!"
Burn my heart with your love,
but stop before I get scorched.

Teach me the amazing truths
I fear to discover.
Feed me the exotic foods
I am afraid to taste.
Offer me the glowing joys
I have denied myself.

Lead me wherever you want
over my personal choices.
Take me to the highest point
beyond my own reach.
Send me into new adventures
wilder than my careful plans.

Help me to grow
taller than my own size.
Stretch me to the breaking point,
past the limits I set.
Test me with challenges
I have previously refused.

Heal me of all my addictions,
even of the ones I like.
Fill me up to the brim
even if I say "Enough!"
Warm my heart with your love,
even if it burns.

Chalin

JM "Are you Mr. and Mrs. Kolichon?"

MsK "Yea."

JM "My name is James McCalmer. I work for the Government.
I am the Director of the Chalin Language Survival Program.
You speak Chalin, don't you?"

MrK "Yea, me and my old lady,
we speak it sixty-one years now,
and a bit English."

JM "You applied for an upgrading English course, didn't you?"

MrK "You mean we want learn English? Yeah."

JM "Unfortunately, you cannot take that course."

MsK "You mean no learn English for us?"

JM "No. Because you are the last two persons
speaking the Chalin language.
If you perfect your English,
we fear that you won't speak Chalin anymore."

MrK "But long time you told us speak only English."

JM "That was years ago.
Now my government is committed
to the survival of the Chalin language."

MsK "Who care? Only us two speaking Chalin now."

JM “We do care a lot.
If you two don’t speak Chalin anymore,
that language will disappear,
and the Chalin Language Survival Program
won’t be needed any more.”

MrK “OK for me.”

JM “Oh no, it’s not OK, because I won’t have a job,
nor my assistant, our clerk, our receptionist,
our two secretaries, and our computer operator.
A disaster in this time of high unemployment.”

MrK “Maybe you make something else survive?”

JM “No, we have been trained specifically
for the survival of the Chalin language.”

MsK “Tikon maolibi gechin, newon English kalikan?”

JM “Excuse me, Mrs. Kolichon, what were you saying?”

MsK “I told my old man, your government,
you pay people to learn speak English.”

JM “Yes, we do.”

MsK “Maybe, I think, your government,
you pay us two to speak only Chalin.”

JM “That’s a great idea!
Yes, we’ll create two positions for you
on the Chalin Language Survival staff.
Would you mind to sign these two forms?”

Mr & MsK Why?”

JM “It reads that you commit yourselves
to speak Chalin from 8 a.m. to 5 p.m.,
every day, five days a week.
Then, our office will pay you a salary.”

MrK “Kalina olinakono.”

JM “Excuse me, Mrs. Kolichon, what did your husband say?”

MsK “My old man, he too, he says OK.”

JM “Thank you so much for your cooperation;
you saved all the jobs in my office.
Goodbye, Mr. and Mrs. Kolichon.”

MsK “Bolino, gominato onimero.”

JM “Excuse me, Mrs. Kolichon, what did you say?
... Oh, don’t bother to translate!
Who cares?”

Celibacy

I will never discuss:

"Will we have a simple wedding, or an extravagant show?"
"Should we rent a house or buy a trailer?"
"Are we to buy a fashionable doll for our five-year-old?"

I will never fear:

"Will we be able to patch it up and start again?"
"Will my wife or I become permanently crippled?"
"What if our young son wants to hitchhike across the U.S.A.?"

I will never worry:

"Will our child survive the night in hospital?"
"Could our daughter have contracted AIDS?"
"Is our son to become a heartless competitor?"

I will never hear:

"Even if you lose your job, I want to move to another town."
"I'm sorry but, as a surgeon, I did everything I could."
"Grandpa, are you going to die?"

Eighty-two Per Cent

Dang Ming had invited his nephew Yao
to leave Nanyang for Edmonton,
and to work in his grocery store on 97th Avenue.

Everything was new for young Yao,
but he mastered computers in one month,
He surfed the Web
and, fond of maths and figures,
he feasted on Canadian statistics:

"Uncle, 235 presidents and vice-presidents
of Canadian corporations
take home a yearly average wage of $449,000,
plus average perks of $93,000."

"Yao, in the seventies,
CEO's made twenty times the industrial wage,
now they make 180 times the industrial average."

"Uncle, in 1994, 81,000 Canadian corporations
made $17.1 billion in profits,
without paying any taxes."

"I remember reading something about that."

"Uncle, look here: In six years,
the wealth of the richest thirty per cent of Canadian families
grew by $7.1 billion
while the bottom fifty per cent of Canadian families
lost $7.3 billion."

"Yes, Yao, *Maclean's* reported that in Toronto,
some families, after paying rent,
live on $3.33 per person, per day,
for food, clothing and other necessities."

"In four years, child poverty rose from fourteen per cent
to twenty per cent.
They say it means 1,472,000 Canadian children."

"Yao, I was told that here in Edmonton
fifty-two per cent of food bank recipients
have gone an entire day without food.
Twenty-one per cent of those who are parents skip meals
so that their children can eat."

"Look, uncle, statistics say that
forty-six per cent of Canadians are Catholics,
and thirty-six per cent, Protestants.
What does that mean, Catholics and Protestants?"

"They are people who follow the Christian religion."

"I never heard of those in China."

"They are named after their leader,
Christ, who lived two thousand years ago."

"What kind of leader was he? What did he say?"

"I was told he preached something like:

'Share everything you have.'
'Give to whomever asks of you.'
Treat everyone as you like to be treated.'
Sell all you have and give the money to the poor.' "

"Uncle, forty-six per cent and thirty-six per cent
makes eighty-two per cent.
Do eighty-two per cent of Canadians follow Christ's teachings?"

"I don't know, Yao.
It sounds strange, doesn't it?"

Marbles

When I was a child,
one side of my house faced *l'impasse du Centre*,
the "dead end alley in the centre of town."
At one place *l'impasse* bulged into a small yard
surrounded by three houses and two garages.
It was surfaced with sand, stones, old mortar,
bits of old bricks and of red roof tiles.
People practised recycling in those days,
even if they didn't talk about it.

Spring didn't start on March 21,
or when flowers started to bloom.
Spring arrived the first day
the schoolyard and *l'impasse*
were dry enough for us to play marbles.
No fancy glass or coloured marbles for us,
our marbles were real marbles, brown, clay marbles.
Most every child also had one 'bomb,'
a one-and-a-half centimetre diameter iron ball
which was allowed in only a few games.

Some days I came back from school,
the pockets of my short pants
bulging with marbles.
My mother shared my pride, but sometimes she added
that the load might rapidly wear out my pockets.
Other days my parents sympathized
with my empty pockets and my heavy heart.

A dozen of us children had adopted
l'impasse for our playground.
During an exciting marble game,
my bomb didn't follow its intended course,
but flew into a neighbour's door.
Tough luck, the door had four glass panels.
Cling, cling, cling ... and the door opened:

"Which one of you did that?"

There were enough witnesses. How could I deny it?

That evening, at supper,
    my dad, as usual, sat at the head of the table.
    and I, on his right:

        "You broke a window in Mr. Bouin's house?"

I had long searched my brain for excuses:
    "Because my bomb hit a stone."
    "Someone pushed me when I was throwing"—
    but not one seemed to be valid.

        "Yes, I did."

Dad handed me a piece of paper:

        "Here are the pane's measurements.
        Tomorrow you will go to Mr. Fonteneau's office
            and tell him to come and replace it."

Did I need to ask the next question?

        "Who will pay for the glass?"

        "You will."

        "I've got no money."

        "You get your weekly allowance.
        You'll save it to pay for the pane."

The earth opened and swallowed me.
I don't recall how many cents or francs it was,
    but on Sundays my parents gave me enough
    to buy a chocolate bar,
    and to go to the children's movie theatre.
How many months or years would it take me?

Mr. Fonteneau was very old. He had some white hair.
His office counter was higher than me,
    but I raised my hand
    and deposited the paper on the counter top.

    "My little boy, who will pay for the glass?'

    "I will, but it will take a while.
    If you trust me ..."

The following Sunday was not a sunny day.
The disaster had happened at the worst of times.
On the previous Sunday the movie theatre
    had shown *Konigsberg,* the best ever mystery,
    filmed in a spooky castle of misty Prussia.
Only the first part of the movie had been shown.
    Goodbye to the second part shown today!

Every Monday I deposited my money on the high counter
    until, one day, the glass man smiled at me:

        "Thank you, my boy. Now it is all paid for."

I jumped and skipped my way back home,
    though still fearful:

        "Did he make a mistake?
        I know that I have paid only half.
        What if he remembers and calls me back?"

My parents had paid the other half.

Builder

My friend Barney and I,
  went to visit our parish priest,
  mostly to see the new rectory
  into which the priest had moved a week before.

The house is stuffed with all kinds of gadgets,
  automatic, electronic and electromagnetic.
I don't like the design, but it's fanciful
  with wide windows, sandblast glass doors,
  a large hallway and an imposing staircase.

It was December 20th.
We walked from the rectory
  to the front of the nearby church.
A few men were building a Jesus stable
  with real wood slabs, two bales of straw,
  plywood people and animals.

As we wandered away from the stable,
Barney looked up into the sky:

> "Dear God, you learned a lot
> about carpentry and building
> in the past two thousand years."

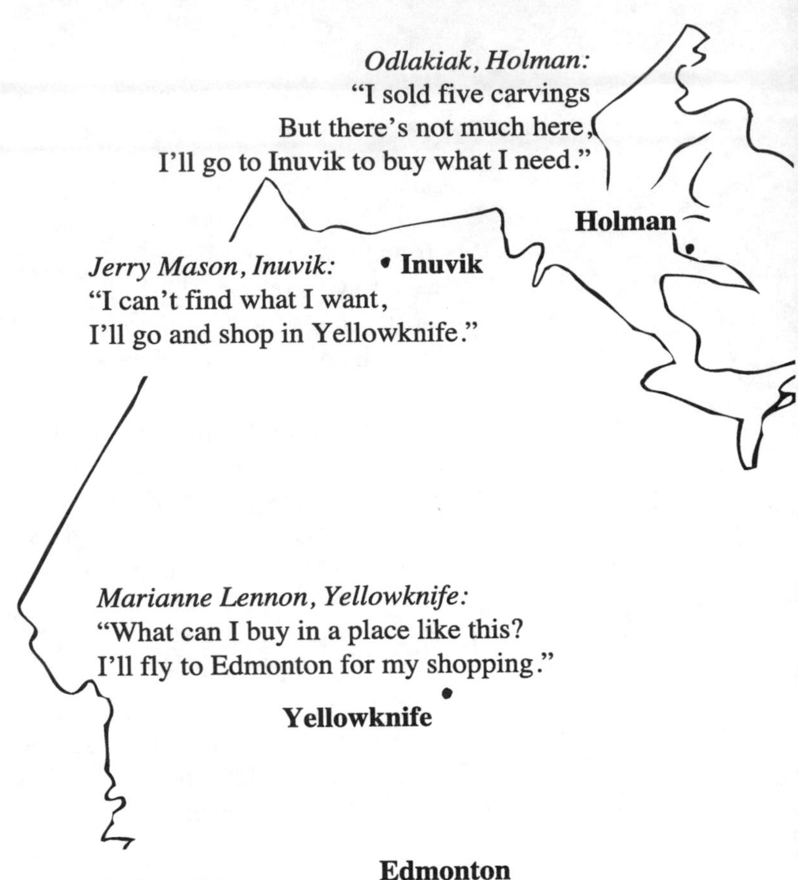

Odlakiak, Holman:
"I sold five carvings
But there's not much here,
I'll go to Inuvik to buy what I need."

Jerry Mason, Inuvik:
"I can't find what I want,
I'll go and shop in Yellowknife."

Marianne Lennon, Yellowknife:
"What can I buy in a place like this?
I'll fly to Edmonton for my shopping."

Berna Collins, Edmonton:
"Kind of a backward country here.
The only place I can shop is Toronto."

Shopping

Ron Graham, Toronto:
"New fashions haven't reached here yet; I'm going to New York to buy proper gifts."
Toronto
New York
Ann Burton, New York:
"My dear, now we are rich, we've made it. Finally, we can afford to purchase Eskimo carvings from Holman."

Dear friend René,

You asked my mother, Tina,
if she had a story to share,
and she says she doesn't have any.
My name is Alex. I am ten years old,
and I want to be a writer,
so here is one of my stories for your book.

No Friend!

"I am really bored in my aquarium
I want some adventure."

Leonardo the turtle swam up,
managed to climb onto the top glass,
jumped out, and fell on the floor:

"What's that?" he said
when he landed on the tail
of a big, sleeping, black cat.

The cat opened his eyes and hissed:

"You spoiled my cat nap!"

Leonardo, afraid, hid in his shell:

"I was looking for a friend,
but I'll have to go back home."

As he crawled slowly on the floor, he wondered:

"How can I get into my aquarium?"

Then he saw some books piled up nearby.
He climbed on them and, still very sad, he jumped in.

"Maybe some day the cat will become kinder,
and be my friend."

Too Independent

Brent: "Excuse me. Are you Fred and Cathy, and do you live here behind the dump?"

Cathy: "That's us, and that's our home."

Brent: "I had to look around for a while to find you. You don't have a lock on your door, so I walked in without knocking."

Fred: "Our friends always walk in without knocking."

Brent: "I don't know if I am one of your friends. City Hall sent me here."

Fred: "Well, good afternoon, sir. By the way, who are you?"

Brent: "I am Mister Brent Lauridan, a by-law enforcement officer."

Cathy: "Welcome, sir. There's tea on the stove. I've got bannock too, and caribou meat."

Brent: "No, thanks. Wait, I'll read you the paper they gave me: 'You must answer my questions with complete sincerity according to your clearest understanding of the facts.' O.K.?

How long have you lived here?"

Cathy: "It's June 1993, so it's about five years."

Brent: "Has your lot been surveyed?"

Fred: "Yes. In winter, our tracks show all the space we use. But you won't see them now in summer time."

Brent: "When you put up that house, did you have a building permit?"

Fred: "I didn't need one. I have my own tools. And I am a good carpenter."

Brent: "Do you have invoices showing where you purchased your building material?"

Fred: "I got lumber, plywood, insulation and roofing paper from the dump over there. The building companies throw away a lot of good stuff."

Brent: "Do you have a separate kitchen and dining room?"

Cathy: "I like to cook outside. I am a good cook. My old man, he likes to eat outside. It's great."

Brent: "Where is your washroom?"

Cathy: "We get water from Fwatsen Creek over there. Also, in summertime we collect rain water, and in winter we melt snow."

Brent: "No! I mean where is your toilet? the powder room? How do you dispose of your human waste?"

Fred: "You mean, shit and stuff like that? We go about fifty yards that way. Three years ago, it was that way, over there. I'll show you that place. It was well fertilized. Now, it's full of flowers, wild roses, buttercups, and fireweed. It's beautiful!"

Brent: "Where is your garbage disposal site?"

Cathy: "Do you have to ask that question?"

Brent: "What is your occupation, your trade, your profession?"

Fred: "We pick up aluminum cans, tin and glass, for recycling."

Brent: "Are you members of a registered recycling operation? Do you have your journeyman's papers? Do you belong to the Chamber of Commerce?"

Fred: "No, but we manage. Some days it works quite well. And we keep the dump from filling up too fast."

Brent: "That may be a problem. City Hall wants the dump to fill up fast so that it has an excuse for spending $3 million on a garbage baler. That's their pet project."

Fred: "Me and my wife, we do the work we can do, and we do it well. We are proud people. We don't want to beg, we don't want to live on welfare."

Brent: "Your lifestyle is dangerous to your health. You live in unsanitary conditions and in violation of the Public Health Act."

Cathy: "Me and my old man, we haven't been in hospital for at least five years."

Brent: "You mean, you never provided any revenue to our hospital? Do you despise the city's modern medical facilities?

Cathy: "You mean the more sick people, the better?"

Brent: "If City Hall sends me to bulldoze your house, will you try to stop me, to punch me, to kick me?"

Fred: "I am not a fighter, I like people."

Brent: "What will you do if I pile up all your belongings, and I burn everything?"

Fred: "I'll watch the flames go up. What would you do if I'd burn your house down?"

Brent: "I'd make sure you go to jail."

Cathy: "Would that help to rebuild your house?"

Brent: "If I burn your house, will you take City Hall to court?"

Fred: "I know them guys at City Hall. I like those people also. Why go to court?"

Brent: "You wouldn't go to court? Do you deny the authority of the justice system? or do you refuse to provide employment to judges, lawyers and prosecutors?"

Cathy: "Us too, we have our good days and our bad days."

Brent: "You cannot stay here. You are too isolated, and the RCMP cannot guarantee your safety."

Fred: "I guess that you are the first person who has ever threatened us."

Brent: “Moreover, the Fire Department couldn’t protect you if there’s a fire in your house.”

Cathy: “So that’s why you want to burn down our house?”

Brent: “You don’t pay for water, you don’t pay for sewage and garbage pickup, you don’t buy building material from our stores. I bet you even get some free food and free clothes from the dump. You are too independent, too self-sufficient.”

Cathy: “Our ancestors lived like that for ten thousand years.”

Brent: “Those days are over. You must be modern, you must depend on politicians, professionals, business people. You set a dangerous example. If many people become self-sufficient as you are, our whole economic system will collapse.”

Fred: “So, what is all your talking about?”

Brent: “It means that your house is nothing but garbage, and we’ll burn it down.”

Fred: “But there is a big sign over there at the dump gate which reads: ‘No Burning of Garbage.’ ”

Brent: “City Hall makes the laws, it doesn’t have to follow them. Goodbye!”

Fred and Cathy: “Goodbye, sir.”

Fred and Cathy pour another cup of tea.

Brent slowly walks away:

“I hate that job. I’m a good man.
I wish I could be free like them.”

A few days later, City Hall burned Fred and Cathy’s house.

Salvation Army

"Ted, have you read those statistics in *News North*?

'In 1989, the Yellowknife Salvation Army provided
2,920 emergency meals,
2,920 shelter beds,
14,000 residential meals,
4,110 daily food line meals,
2,659 care days to people on parole, to young offenders,
and to inmates of the Correctional Centre.'"

"They surely do good work.
Nobody else could manage those programs.
I'm glad they are going to build a larger building."

"I had never heard of that.
They really need a bigger place.
Where are they going to build?"

"At the corner of Franklin Avenue and 45th Street."

"45th Street! That's my street.
I don't want that kind of people on my street;
beggars, drunkards, young offenders.
We are a good neighbourhood.
City Hall will hear from us.
I'll mobilize the whole street against them."

P.B.P.

The directors of P.B.P.
met in their boardroom
in January 1992

"You have read the 1991 financial report. Good news from all our properties. Sales were up twenty-two per cent. Profit up thirty-four per cent. The Becalan mine proved to be a real windfall: $845 million."

"Thank you, Russell, for those details. Now, I would like to hear from the exploration department."

"The final report on our Lamar property will be ready in two weeks. A promising report, and we'll open a mine there in spring, 1994. On the other side of the world, we sent a geological survey crew to the Northwest Territories."

"That's in Canada, isn't it?"

"Yes, Raimundo, it's north of Toronto and of Vancouver."

"What did we discover?"

"Appalling conditions! Our crew camped near a village called Dreg Lake where unemployment is sixty-five per cent. There's no highway to that place, and all the freight has to be flown in. Prices for milk and vegetables at the local store are sky high. No swimming pool up there, no golf course, not even a shooting range. The nearby lake is magnificent, but there's not one cruise ship, not even a sailboat. The school has only old 1988 computers. Nobody wears gold or diamond jewelry."

"Abelard, it looks like you want to say something. You've been the longest with the company, you're our respected elder, so you speak first. How do you feel?"

"We have to help those poor people. We'll build a five-thousand-foot airstrip there to bring tourists and to boost the local economy. We will also build a road from Dreg Lake to wherever is the next city. Supplies will get there cheaper."

"But Abelard, an airstrip and a road would cost $50 million. Can we afford that?"

"Whatever the cost, we have to. That's our name and our motto: P.B.P."

"Walker, what else did we discover there?"

"Ten kimberlite pipes. All of them are certainly studded with diamonds. And there are definitely many more pipes to be discovered."

"So, if we build a highway for the people of Dead? Dread? yes, Dreg Lake, we could also use that road to move equipment to our mine. And we could use the airstrip to fly workers from the South."

"But wherever we open a mine, it is primarily to provide employment for the local people."

"Oh yes, Abelard, we'll find jobs for them, but you understand that mining is no more a pick and shovel operation. It will be easy to establish a mine near Dreg Lake: dam three rivers, drain five lakes, level a few hills, fill up a valley, that's all."

"But will the local people agree to those changes?"

"You know, Rosenthal, not all the people have to agree. Most don't know much of anything. Some still believe that diamonds are mined like gold. I am sure that we can befriend a few local leaders to our side. We'll impress them with free trips around the world to show them our properties. Such trips won't cost us more than $300,000."

"Is there a government up there?"

"Yes, but it's a young, mini-government, nothing similar to the American states or the Canadian provinces."

"Can we make deals with that government?"

"That government doesn't know how to foster business initiatives or to create local employment. With the jobs we create, some benefits will trickle down to that government, and its leaders will approve whatever we do."

"We really have to open those mines, to help those poor people and that poor government."

"Thank you, Abelard, for your approval."

"By the way, those ventures will also profit our company. We expect that a twenty-year mining operation will bring us $10 billion. That's a conservative estimate."

"Whatever our profits or our losses, we have to remember our motto: P.B.P. We have to help those people and that government in ... where is that again?"

"In the Northwest Territories. But Abelard, why do you always mention our motto?"

"It's important! We must follow our motto: P.B.P.— 'People Before Profit.' "

"Abelard, our motto is P.B.P.— 'Profit before People.' "

"Oh? Is it? I'm sorry, Excuse me, you know that I'm getting old. Sometimes I get a bit confused."

Les Palmes académiques

My book, *As Long as This Land Shall Last,*
was published in 1975.

The French consul in Edmonton congratulated me
that a Frenchman
had contributed so much to the history of the Dene:
"Could you please send me your curriculum vitae
and more details about yourself and your life,
since I want to propose your name
for *Les Palmes académiques*?"

Les Palmes académiques is a French decoration.

"Dear Mr. Consul," I answered,

"I've been living with the Dene for over 20 years.
We have tried to help each other in many ways,
and we had a great time together. At least I did.
I feel happy that my work also brings glory to France,
but I don't see how a medal could make me
a better person, a better friend, or a better Frenchman.
May I suggest that, instead of a medal, you send me
a return plane ticket from Yellowknife to Paris,
so that I can visit my mother and my brothers?"

Guess what I received?
No medal, no plane ticket!

Fishing

In 1960, Great Bear Fishing Lodge opened
    on the east end of Sahtu (Great Bear Lake).
U.S. fisherfolk, eager for trophies,
    marvelled at the 40- or 50-pound lake trout.

To test their skill at grayling fishing,
    some chartered a small plane for a day
    to Délı̨ne (Fort Franklin), 200 kilometres to the west.
Délı̨ne is near the outlet of Sahtu,
    where graylings thrive
    in the swift water of Sahtú Dıé (Bear River).

Wide-eyed tourists also took time
    to wander through the village,
    survey the houses and tepees,
    and observe the Dene way of life.

Winter is trapping and hunting time for the Dene.
Rivers, lakes and muskegs are frozen,
    and become paths, trails, or highways.
Summertime is more relaxed,
    with easy canoe or boat travel.
The few warm days chase away all worries
    about gathering firewood or making fire,
    dressing and undressing children.

The tourist fisherfolk wondered endlessly
at a way of life they never suspected to exist:

"You people surely don't live like we do."

"Like what?"

"We work hard for twenty or thirty years,
and we save our money."

"What for?"

"When we have enough money in the bank,
we can retire."

"What do you do when you retire?"

"We don't have to work,
we visit friends when we feel like it,
we go fishing when we feel like it."

The Dene looked more perplexed than the tourists.

Election Campaign

Canada destroyed the aboriginal political institutions
which had lasted ten thousand years.
Then, it refused the right to vote
to aboriginal men living on reserves until 1960,
and to aboriginal women until 1968.
The Dene were allowed to vote earlier.
They didn't live on reserves.

In May 1957, a candidate for the Conservative Party,
three-piece suit, shiny shoes, fashionable hat,
flew in to Rádęlį Kǫ́ (Fort Good Hope).

"I want to hold a meeting."

"We like meetings."

"In which location?"

"There's a community hall down there."

"What would be the most appropriate time?"

"Right now."

Soon, a few dozen people were sitting
on the hall's floor, along the walls.

"I need an interpreter."

"George there is the best one."

"Ladies and gentlemen, next month,
you will have the honour and the privilege
to exercise your franchise ...

Please, can you translate?"

"Can you say it again?"

"Ladies and gentlemen, next month ..."

"That's OK, can you say something else?"

All the something else which followed
was really *something else* for the Dene.
Every time the candidate spoke for three minutes,
the interpreter spoke for three minutes.
Two minutes for one, two minutes for the other.
For a long, long time, the Dene listened politely.
Everyone clapped and the meeting was over.

A week later, Merv Hardie,
the candidate for the Liberal party, showed up,
shaking the same hands, speaking at the same location,
to the same audience.
Merv sat on the floor like everyone else:

"OK, boys, June 10, there will be an election.
It means that there will be two names on a paper,
my name is on top, and the other guy's name is below.
With a cross you'll show who is the better one.
I've been around here for a long time.
You know me, I know you.
All of you S.O.B.'s, you better vote for me!"

Clapping! Clapping! Meeting is over.

Merv Hardie got sixty-nine votes,
the other candidate, four.

Christmas Tree

"Bill, did you read today's newspaper?
    The Federal Government
        has devised a new program
        to benefit all Canadian Indians."

"No, René, I haven't seen it.
    Another Christmas tree policy?"

"What Christmas tree are you talking about?"

"Well, every December,
    white people go to the bush,
    cut down a beautiful tree,
    prop it up in their living room,
    decorate it with candy canes,
    plastic birds and coloured lights.
They admire the tree, show it off,
    praise it, sing to it, and oh and ah!"

"It's true, some trees are pretty."

"For how long?
Three weeks later,
    the glorious tree is cast out to the dump.
You know why, René? Because they cut off its roots.
Same thing with government programs.
For a while, they decorate the Indians
    with tinsel and flashing lights.
But every program cuts off more of our roots.
No wonder we always land at the dump."

Addiction

"Tanya, why do addicts return again and again
to what they have done before?"

"I guess they can't relate to the real world,
and they feel secure only with old routines."

"Why do they close all doors
between themselves and the rest of society?"

"Addicts look for simple solutions to life.
They create artificial relationships
within their own minds, with each other,
and with the whole of creation."

"Whether an experience is a good one or a bad one,
they seem to simply need it."

"They can't appreciate each other's qualities,
so they merely repeat previous patterns."

"Do they rely on externals
to block out their own feelings?"

"Most addicts probably don't like their addiction,
but they use it to avoid facing their fears."

"Don't they feel the need to assert themselves
and to be responsible for their own lives?"

"Wally, a lot of people may not even know
that alternatives exist."

"But the more often addicts get together,
with no personal strength to share,
the more dependency they create for each other."

“And the less they are able to leave their pack.”

“But Tanya, you never drank too much, you never shot drugs. How did you learn about addiction?”

“I wasn’t talking about booze and drugs.”

“I mean, in your past, were you addicted to something?”

“Yes, for twenty years I was addicted to religion.”

Goodbye

Jean Amourous, born in 1925 on the French-Italian border,
started life with two mother tongues.
He joined the Oblates of Mary Immaculate,
and was ordained priest in 1951.
A year later, he arrived in Denendeh,
and got his first, and last, posting to Bèchokǫ̀ (Rae).
We used to call him 'Grand Jean'
as he was taller than the other Jean
who stayed with him for years.
With his musical ear, and innate determination,
Grand Jean rapidly learned English,
and mastered the Dogrib language,
then spoken by every Tłįchǫ (Dogrib),
in their very traditional communities.

The Dogribs enjoy recounting many stories
lived by Grand Jean in their villages,
or during his many winter trips by dog-team
between Bèchokǫ̀, Gamètı (Rae lake),
Wekwetı (Snare Lake), and Wha Tı (Lac la Martre).
Summer time saw him with the Tlinchon
on many lakes, rivers and portages.

Grand Jean's joy was contagious;
he was free to love, free to serve, free to help.
He usually travelled with his packsack
full of dried meat to be delivered to one and all.
His pockets regularly bulged
with pieces of paper or of cardboard,
an unending list of errands
he had offered to run.

A few years ago, we noticed that
Grand Jean floundered more and more:

"I got to ... eu ... Bertha's house,
and ... eu ... Larry, ... no, Gerry,
he was back from ... eu ..."

Alzheimer's disease was invading Grand Jean's brain.

The Dogribs showed every possible kindness to him
and pleaded with the Church authorities
that he remain with them in Bèchokǫ̀.
But, by 1991, Grand Jean needed more attention,
and he was invited to retire at Placid Place,
an Oblate residence in Edmonton.

Lee, a friend, offered to chauffeur Grand Jean
one hundred kilometres from Bèchokǫ̀ to Yellowknife,
where he could catch a flight to Edmonton.
Grand Jean sat silently in the car,
without any sign of emotion,
whether aware or not that he was leaving
Bèchokǫ̀ and his Dogrib friends for ever.

About half way to Yellowknife,
a big smile came to Grand Jean's face:

"Stop ... stop ... stop ...!"

He opened the door,
walked a few steps alongside the road,
resolutely veered to the right,
and tramped through the muskeg.
Lee froze:

"What can I do?
Scream? Blow the horn?
or simply trust and hope?"

A burly black bear and her young cub
    were plodding their way towards Grand Jean
    who started to whistle softly at them.
Soon, he and the bears faced each other,
    and carried on a lengthy conversation.

Once the three friends had said their goodbye,
    the bears serenely shuffled away,
    and Grand Jean headed back towards the car.
He opened the door, and calmly sat down.

Lee wiped away a tear and started the car.